AF574793

A Bee in the Kitchen

H. F. Ellis is perhaps best known as the creator of that ineffable prep school master, Arthur James Wentworth, familiar to readers of *A. J. Wentworth, B.A.* (and its recent sequel *Swan Song of A. J. Wentworth*) – as also to radio listeners and to those who saw Arthur Lowe in his final television role.

H. F. Ellis has also been writing elegant and witty pieces for *Punch* and later *The New Yorker* and other magazines for over half a century. Here is a vintage collection of the best of his work – light essays, articles, parodies and 'episodes' – from the past twenty years. The range of topics he covers is wide, including bees, butlers, the extinction of dinosaurs, Greek plays and cormorants, the origins of man and of the universe and even TV cookery. The whole is a richly entertaining mélange of stylish meditations, eloquent evocations of human predicaments that one recognises with delight and hilarious flights of fancy that may sometimes make the reader laugh aloud.

'Mr Ellis has the rare knack of taking a subject and shrouding it in a light cocoon of asides and literary allusions to make a delightfully frothy whole. We . . . leave the book refreshed by Mr Ellis's lively and wide-ranging wit.' *The Lady by the same author*

A.J. WENTWORTH BA
SWAN SONG OF A.J. WENTWORTH

A Bee in the Kitchen

And Other Distractions

H.F. ELLIS

METHUEN

A Methuen Paperback

First published in Great Britain 1983
The paperback edition first published 1984
by Methuen London Ltd
11 New Fetter Lane, London EC4P 4EE

ISBN 0 413 54530 X (paperback)

Phototypeset by Tradespools Ltd, Frome, Somerset
Made and printed in Great Britain by
Richard Clay (The Chaucer Press) Ltd, Bungay, Suffolk

Contents

Acknowledgements

Much of the material in this book first appeared in *The New Yorker* and I am indebted to the proprietors for permission to reprint it here.

Other pieces were published in *Punch*, *The Countryman* and *The Atlantic*. To these magazines also I extend my grateful acknowledgements.

Introduction

Having dealt at some length on a later page with Introductions as an art form I am inclined to keep this one mercifully short. Here then is a selection or collation, not hitherto presented in book form, of what seemed to me the better of the innumerable light essays and other trivia I have written during the two decades from 1960 to 1980. Some two-thirds of the material had its first airing in the United States and is therefore likely to be unfamiliar, though not necessarily incomprehensible, to British readers.

The order in which these pieces appear can only be described as haphazard. It is certainly not chronological, but any reader who cares to trace the author's development, or lack of it, over the twenty years here represented will find the original publication date – as also an indication of its provenance – appended to each title in the table of Contents. Where (in two cases) no such information is provided, it may be taken that the articles have not previously appeared anywhere and are included as an act of defiance to the editor or editors who failed to appreciate their worth. A date has also been added here and there in the text, where the flight of time seemed to make it advisable in the interests of clarity.

These essays were written at intervals, long or short, and should be read, I suggest, in the same way – though not, perhaps, over a period of twenty years.

Moment of Truth for a Small Man

The pub in which I found myself was not, either in its outward or inward aspect, at all remarkable. It simply happened to lie on the route from the place where I had been to the place where I was going, and to coincide with the moment when I felt that a rapid sherry would be acceptable. There were people in the bar, but not in such numbers as to make me reconsider my decision. Two minutes, I reckoned, would see me on my way again; and so it would have turned out, had not a newcomer shouldered me aside so rudely as I was drinking that a good shillingsworth of dry Fino was jerked out of the glass.

I was now face to face with a situation that men of large physique know nothing about. Dabbing a lapel with my handkerchief I considered the side view of this insolent aggressor. His nearer shoulder, hunched up by the forearm that rested hugely on the bar, rose like the north face of the Eiger, obscuring most of the massive face, but the flushed and furrowed brows suggested drink or ill-temper, or both. Across his back the dark blue coat was strained to the point of audibility. The hand, a little mottled, that reached out to enfold a pint of stout bore bone-crushing rings on its middle fingers. The question I had to decide was whether or not to take up the matter of my spilt sherry.

One can say 'What's the idea – pushing in like that?' and wait for the slow turning of the head, the astonished enlargement of the sodden eyes, the almost incredulous

'You talking to *me*?' There is no difficulty about that part of it. But where is it going to get you? Not to an apology; because this kind of blundering hooligan doesn't apologise. To what then? To words? To all the indignity and futility of swapped abuse, of quivering pomposities like 'Don't you speak to me like that, my man!' rattling ineffectually against such impenetrable vulgarities as '*Get* aht, yer silly little turkeycock!' Or to a sudden backhanded swipe, with benefit of rings? Or worse? What does it prove, tell me that, to be lifted clean off one's feet by the coat-front and then hurled across the bar like some bounty-hunter in a Western? 'Admitted to Charing Cross Hospital after a public-house brawl, and believed to be suffering from a fractured skull. . . .'

The wise, the dignified, the only possible course is to ignore provocative rudeness altogether. And yet, I asked myself, continuing to mop my clothes in a dark and concentrated way like a coiled spring that may at any instant unleash itself – and yet, suppose some smaller man, some littlish bouncy bottle-necked solicitor, say, had come barging in and drenched me in my own refreshment, would I have settled for silence, for a policy of dignified non-expostulation in face of such brazen, such deliberate loutishness? I thought not. I doubted it very much. So then it was a question of comparative size; or at best of convincing myself that it was *not* a question of size. A vision of Mr Polly flashed across my mind: of Mr Polly sitting by the wayside, three miles from the Potwell Inn, trying desperately to persuade himself that the right, the sensible thing to do about the ugly and ferocious Uncle Jim was to go right away, to keep on walking eastward and never come back. Mr Polly did so persuade himself – but he turned westward all the same, along the perilous route that his tiresome manhood bade him take.

On the other hand, of course, Mr Polly had much

more at stake. There was the fat woman to defend.

This dilemma was resolved for me by the aggressor himself, who, perhaps becoming aware of a concentrated gaze upon the back of his neck, turned massively round and said:

'Something troubling you, matey?'

I said there was, and told him about it. I told him all about it. It seems extraordinary, in retrospect, that I should have laid the whole problem before this unappetising stranger, but that is what I did. I told him of the difficulties of the smaller man. I asked him, passionately, to consider what it must be like either to do nothing in the face of provocation, and be self-convicted of cowardice, or to do something, and get nowhere – perhaps to be gripped by the collar and tie, and lifted into the air, kicking like a rabbit; to have to make the choice between being a private craven or a public mockery. 'How would you like that?' I asked him. I demanded, in my keyed-up state, to be told whether he thought it fair.

He listened gravely, giving his whole attention to a problem that had perhaps never been put to him before. His great forefinger traced circles in a pool of beer on the counter, and a sort of indignation darkened his dull and yellowish eyes.

'Somebody been bothering you, then?' he asked.

'I was standing with this glass in my hand,' I began, 'quietly minding my—'

'Big man, eh?' he said. 'In here, is he?'

There are depths of stupidity, nadirs of crass incomprehension, against which one has no defences. I looked wildly round the bar, seeking courage perhaps to attempt again the hurdle I thought I had already cleared, to say in so many words 'It was *you*,' and the mottled man, following my agonised gaze, caught sight of another and even larger man sitting peacefully drinking bitter at a table.

'I see 'im,' he said, and putting a hand protectively on my shoulder, in a gesture you might see in some funeral stele from Athens, propelled me across the room. 'No,' I said. 'Listen—' But his time for listening was over.

'What's the idea, then?' he demanded of the bitter drinker, whose name registered on my mind, with the inconsequence that often accompanies crisis, as Chief Sitting Bull. 'Pushing this little feller around!'

Sitting Bull merely looked at my champion with untroubled loathing, the sort of look one might give a snake known to have had its fangs removed, and looked away again. He had a trace of stubble on his chin and wore a thick sweater with Christmas trees worked on it.

'It wasn't,' I began. 'This gentleman had nothing—'

'Up!' the mottled man said briefly. 'On your feet, boy.'

Nobody took any notice of my protests at all. Sitting Bull gazed moodily into his beer for perhaps a couple of seconds, then rose with alarming suddenness and laid a vast hand on my champion's waistcoat. 'Off!' he said. 'Go and find Nanny.' One of his Christmas trees was a little out of alignment: a homely touch that somehow heightened the nightmare quality of this gigantic confrontation.

I think the mottled man took half a pace backwards at this point. Or perhaps he was pushed. At any rate he jogged the arm of a man behind him, who instantly pushed him forward again, with objurgations, so violently that Sitting Bull rocked visibly on his foundations. I knew now exactly how it would be. One push leads to another. Chair legs were without doubt already being loosened in readiness all round the bar. I have seen this kind of thing a dozen times on *Z Cars* and elsewhere, and if there is one thing that stands out more clearly than another it is that interference from bystanders does no manner of good at all. It only complicates matters.

So I went away. Dull thuds followed me as I gained

the street, and a little later I thought I heard the shrill note of a police whistle. I felt saddened by the turn of events, but wiser. I had learned a lesson, invaluable for the smaller man, that one should always let provocation from bigger men pass by. It is not a question of cowardice. It is simply that, if a rumpus results, it is the big men who will get hurt. One ought not to ask it of them.

Without Whose Unfailing Encouragement

For the genesis of my book, 'An Introduction to the Study of Introductions,' I am principally indebted to my psychiatrist, Dr Adolphus Peters, of Amsterdam. Having occasion to consult him about an irritating obsessive compulsion, which took the form of an inability to skip the introductory pages of any serious work that fell into my hands, I was at first repelled by his suggestion that instead of resisting the compulsion I embrace it and, by making a careful analysis of these preliminary throat-clearings, get them, in his homely phrase, out of my system. He persisted, however. Imagination gradually took fire, and now, some fifteen years later, it is a pleasure as well as a duty to record my gratitude to one but for whom I might still be unable to get as far as Chapter I of any book, not least my own.

A brief explanation is necessary to delineate the limits I have set myself in this inquiry. Forewords, not being in general the work of the writers whose books they seek to illumine or confute, I decided to omit, except insofar as they are referred to with gratification (see Chapter 9 *passim*) by the actual authors in their Introductions. The Prefatory Note has, of course, already been the subject of a scholarly monograph by Herr Emil Strohler, while the history and development of Contents (including List of Plates) will always be associated with the name of Silas R. Wisehammer, of Wisconsin. On these well-tilled fields I had no wish to trespass. Surprisingly little attention appears to have been paid to the Introduction proper, even the Germans having contented themselves with some rather cursory statistics, without any attempt to evaluate Introductions as an art form or to inquire into density of readership, recurrent phraseology, the omission quotient, and kindred matters of importance to the prolegomenist. I make no apology therefore for attempting to fulfil a want so ably categorised by Miss Phyllis Ashbaker, BSC (who has given freely of her storehouse of specialised knowledge in a Foreword to this volume that I can never hope adequately to acknowledge), as 'long felt'.

Particular attention has been paid to Acknowledgements, since these form at once the most universal and the least understood feature of Introductions. Of some 87,000 persons individually thanked for their help in the 5,319 Introductions it has been my good fortune to read and analyse, I have been in touch with rather more than half – a labour of love that seemed to me essential, as it is from their ranks that the Introduction readership proved to be almost totally drawn. I desire to thank them all again here, but have been compelled, in order to avoid over-weighting this Introduction, to take the unorthodox course of relegating their names to Appendix III. (No such comprehensive list of generous advisers, unstinting critics, laborious proofreaders, owners of hitherto unpublished mss. to which they most kindly gave me access, and patient wives, drawn from every field of life and learning, from the preparation of soufflés to a new interpretation of the Gilgamesh Epic, has, it is believed, ever been compiled before.)* If I single out Dr Wilbur H. Gumshott, of the Institute of Anthropology in Boston, it is only because

*This parenthesis took the form of a footnote in my original draft, but it was unsparingly pointed out to me by Mr Wilberforce Butt OBE**, who most generously read through the greater part of these preliminary pages, that the use of footnotes in Introductions is atypical – except for such unavoidable addenda as e.g.

**Now Sir Wilberforce Butt, KBE

the telephone conversation I had with him well illustrates the invaluable side-lights on my subject afforded me by personal contact with many helpers.

MYSELF: Have I the good fortune to be speaking to, or with, Dr Wilbur H. Gumshott, who gave unstintingly of his unrivalled insight into Peruvian wedding rites during the preparation of Chapter 17 of Mildred Worthington's *South American Rhapsody*?

DR G: Who *is* this?

MYSELF: I have been entrusted, though fully conscious that there must be many better qualified both by—

DR G: Are you aware, sir, whoever you are, that it is three o'clock in the morning, Eastern Standard Time?

MYSELF: I trust it is not an inconvenient moment. The fact is that I have already made calls in the same connection to your colleagues Professor T.R. McGluskey, Mr Alfred Bains, Mr Aloysius Mannering, and Dr Bernard Hackslip, as well as to Miss Freda Staring, the acknowledged authority on the Puelche of Araucania, and to the librarian of the School of Amer-Indian Studies in Beirut, but for whose unfailing encouragement and advice—

DR G: That bunch! What Hackslip knows about Peru wouldn't cover half a file card.

MYSELF: Thank you. That certainly sheds fresh light. I see, however, that the acknowledgment to him and the other colleagues I have mentioned begins 'I am particularly grateful', whereas for yourself and Professor Richard A. Butterstone, of Halifax, Nova Scotia, the phrase 'I also desire to thank' was deemed appropriate. May I have your comments on that?

DR G: I have nothing to say.

MYSELF: Bearing in mind that the even warmer 'I owe a very great debt of gratitude' is reserved for Miss Mabel Gilchrist on page 9—

DR G: Never heard of her.

MYSELF: She gave invaluable assistance with the typing, thus taking her place on my secretarial ranking list second only to those eleven hundred and forty-eight devoted women whose untiring skill and patience in unravelling what was often, the authors fear, a sadly illegible—

DR G: Why don't you bother the people who write all this rubbish, and leave me alone? I have to get some sleep.

The question raised by Dr Gumshott is of some importance. I did, of course, apply direct to some thousands of authors whose prolegomenorrhea (the word was coined for me by my friend Charlie Pyke, BA, who also drew my attention to the delicate interplay of colon and semicolon in a brilliant list of helpers cited by an otherwise obscure Swedish geophysicist) had brought them within my purview, but the response was not uniformly encouraging. This despite the fact that I was able in many cases to inform them of points of interest of which they themselves appeared to be unaware. Thus, I was the first to advise Mr Karl Strummholtz that in singling out for special mention in the Introduction to his 'Volcanoes in Antiquity' no less than seventy-five friends and colleagues, fifteen universities or other institutes, the mother superior of a nunnery, three typists, his publisher, five proofreaders, and both his first and second wives (who 'cheerfully bore') he had established a record for scientific works outside the field of ornithology. Others had not even troubled to reflect that, by removing their acknowledgments to a separate section headed 'Acknowledgments', they ran the risk of reducing their Introduction readership to nil, apart from psychopaths like myself. In volunteering information, in their turn, I found writers uncooperative to such a degree that I feel unable to thank more than three hundred and seventy of them by name. (Appendix IV.) To a simple written questionnaire requesting answers to such inquiries as

In the preparation of your Introductions, by what authors have you been especially influenced; e.g. as to style, presentation, addition of '*Majorca, 1967*' at the end, etc?

Have you acknowledged this debt?

Who *is* this Lady Alice Brackenbury who so kindly translated the Chinese quatrain on page 196?

What do you mean, exactly, by 'unsparing'?

For every half-dozen colleagues gratified by a mention, how many took immortal umbrage from (a) total omission, or (b) the 'lumping' technique?

most authors did not bother to reply. Of those who did, a disappointingly high proportion complained that only the preliminary pages of their books appeared to have been read. This attitude, as between specialists, struck me as inexplicable.

It only remains to add that in the final stages of this work I have been sustained by the Vicar, by a certain Mrs Potter (or possibly Cotter), of Exeter, who, in the act of measuring my settee for a new slipcover, inadvertently or intentionally made off with three pages from Chapter 2, and by so indefatigable an army of other critics that I have reluctantly been forced to hold their names over to an additional Appendix (V). Nevertheless, any errors and omissions remain entirely mine, and for this sole residuum of my labours I am profoundly grateful.

The Channel Islands,
Wednesday

Sun and Wine

The rays of the afternoon sun, striking through my glass, made a small pool of light on the tablecloth. It was late May in Italy, so there was nothing remarkable about that. But I watched it. The upper arc of the sloping, fan-shaped Campo in Siena, with the ridiculous and enchanting tower of the Palazzo Pubblico bursting into a stony efflorescence at the top of its plain brick stem across there on the southern side, offers as fair an after-luncheon prospect as any that has been granted to me. One could sit there just looking at it, as I don't doubt generations of tourists have told each other, for ever. Still, for the time being I was looking at this pool of sunlight on the tablecloth. The light was of course refracted, though I would not care to say (not knowing the refractive index of Chianti) how much, and it occurred to me that this was a strange and, in a way, a rather pitiful thing. For ninety-three million miles those rays had come hurtling, straight as a die through bleak and chartless regions to the very square yard of Tuscan territory that was briefly mine; and then, at the very last infinitesimal fraction of time, within a bare three inches of their ultimate goal, had been savagely wrenched and twisted out of true. It seemed hard.

I would not claim that my enjoyment of the mellow scene was imperilled. One does not get seriously sentimental about rays of light, except perhaps at weddings in cathedrals. On the contrary, I was pleased with my thought – not a profound thought when set down in cold print on a colder day, but rich and somehow right in sunshine in Siena – and when the waiter came to recommend yet more of his splendid wine from Castellina I felt a strong desire to share it. Abroad on holiday, and nowhere else, one is at liberty to philosophise with strangers.

'You see this spot?' I said, putting a lazy forefinger on the tablecloth.

He flicked at it with his napkin, a purely reflex action; and equally instinctively, my mind still busy, I suppose, with the immensity of the journey that had brought that fleck of radiance to the table, I cried, 'Don't *do* that!'

'Sir?' he said.

'Bent,' I said. 'Right at the finish. After all that.' And I tapped the glass once or twice, to help him. 'Your wine,' I said, smiling to show that I was *simpatico*, 'affects even the sun.'

'Vino,' he agreed, and went away.

Dreamily observing the gentle sweep of the buildings on my side of the Campo I reflected that space, too, is curved. The sun's rays had not perhaps come to me absolutely straight; they might even have been pulled a little this way or that by the attraction of some intrusive planet or asteroid. Still, the basic validity of my thought was not impaired. I need not bother the waiter with Einstein.

'I only meant,' I explained, when he returned, a little tentatively, with more Chianti, 'the light, *luce*, comes *mille miglia* no, *millione*. Straight. *Diritto*.' I pointed at the sun and then, with a gesture a child could have understood, drew my finger down in a dead straight line until it rested on the rim of my glass, which the waiter immediately refilled. '*Diritto*,' I said again. 'And then, look! *Fratturata*!'

'Excuse,' he said.

I saw him talking in the voluble Italian way to a senior colleague, now pointing with exaggerated emphasis at the sky, now prodding despondently at a nearby tablecloth. His shoulders rose in the air, and I began to despair of philosophising with strangers. But his colleague was not for a moment at a loss. He came at speed, dynamic and in complete control, bearing one of those large umbrellas.

'*Molto caldo*,' he said, and blotted out for good and all my little pool of refracted light. 'So,' he said, with many smiles.

I could not tell what would happen to my baffled rays. Would they be reflected, bounce back at a multitude of angles from that gay domed surface, voyage onwards and outwards again on their altered paths for millions and millions of years, perhaps have lost for ever their chance of making a little brilliant spot of focused and refracted light in the loveliest city in the world? I thought it probable, and said. But I did not weep. One does not weep easily in Siena.

A Bee in the Kitchen

1979

The thing began at Olympia, a large exhibition hall in London more often devoted to Show Jumping but on this occasion the scene of a tennis World Doubles Championship. The British pair, curly-haired Cox and his partner, Lloyd, were playing McEnroe and Fleming for a place in the finals, and at one time, with the score at 3-all in the last set and a service break not inconceivable, looked as though, against all the odds, they might win. They did not, and I switched off the television and went to the kitchen for some ice. A bee was buzzing about in there – not a usual event in a cold English January, so I spoke to it. 'We lost!' I told it bitterly.

Of the two kinds of insanity exhibited here I reckon that the bitterness was the more extreme. 'Telling the bees' is an old English custom, still practised, I believe, in the remoter rural districts of the West Country. This courtesy is, or was, usually extended in the event of a death in the family – the proper procedure being to tap the hive three times, repeating 'So-and-So is dead' at each tap. The penalty for failure to make this announcement is another death in the household within the year, or, as some say, the departure of the bees to some other and more communicative locality. Of course, a solitary bee is not a hive and cannot easily be tapped; but there is at least a precedent for giving the news to bees, and, for all we know, they may be as interested in one kind of disaster as another. What concerns me more deeply is that I should, even momentarily, regard the loss of a tennis match as disastrous.

Tennis is not a game that greatly excites me *per se*, nor one that I ever played much above the level at which a start is made with five balls because the sixth went into the laurel hedge last Sunday. Cox and Lloyd, though British, were not playing *for* Britain, and if they had been, their success could have reflected no conceivable credit on me personally. They were playing for a top prize of twenty thousand pounds each – a reward, for a few days' serving and returning, so ridiculously out of proportion as to fill me, in my saner moods, with nausea and despair. What kind of distorted patriotism, nationalism, chauvinism is this that makes me care tuppence whether a backhand crosscourt volley with heavy top spin did or did not land one inch outside the line and that drives me untimely into the kitchen to cry out 'We lost!' to a solitary out-of-season bee. Who is 'we' for God's sake?

It is useless, as a matter of fact, to tell bees anything. They can't hear. I ought to have known that, because when writing, years ago, about Gilbert White and the effect of echoes on bees,* I quoted a passage in which that capable eighteenth-century naturalist denies that the creatures respond in any way to sounds. He proved it for himself by roaring at them through a speaking trumpet held close to their hive and noting that they failed to show 'the least sensibility or resentment.' Perhaps he should have tapped first, to gain their attention, though I doubt whether it would have made any difference. All that I have read about bees – and I have read a good deal since that discreditable incident in the kitchen – seems to show that you need a special technique to get any message through to them.

Take Sir John Lubbock, for instance – not the distinguished astronomer 'J.W.' but his son, a considerable scientist in his own right and a keen bee-watcher, who, about a century after Gilbert White, was hard at it on the same old tack of trying to make himself

* See, in due course, 'For a Gentleman of Fortune' on page 57.

heard. Aware that, on occasion, a new queen in the hive sets up an intermittent piping, to which any residual young queens appear to respond, he naturally asked himself what was the point of this exchange of sounds if neither party could hear them. They might as well be discussing Home Rule in Parliament. Nevertheless, Sir John was unable to get his bees to take any notice of any sound he could devise, and in the end, reluctant to believe that all this piping was to no avail, fell back on the supposition that they could only hear higher notes than any at his personal disposal.

Now take another great leap forward, this time of half a century or more, and see what Karl von Frisch, the *Dancing Bees* man, has to say. He will have none of this 'higher note' shilly-shallying. To the duet within the hive he readily admits. 'The free queen,' he says, 'emits a kind of piping sound and the imprisoned queens also make similar noises which, however, from the depth of their dungeons sound like a hollow "quack quack",' and he goes on to tell us how 'Bee-keepers maintain that the quacking bees are asking whether there is a queen about, and as long as they get an answering piping, they take good care not to leave the protection of their cells.' They know very well, you see, that she will not tolerate any rivals. This sounds like good bee sense to me, but it won't do for von Frisch. Bees, he states categorically, 'are unable to distinguish between piping and quacking' – and how I wish I had been around while he was proving *that* to his own satisfaction – 'and are only receptive to tones in their immediate vicinity through a very finely developed sense of touch.'

So there we are. Had I known all this before entering the kitchen I should never have dreamed of trying to share my patriotic distress with a bee. Even if you take the side of the beekeepers against von Frisch and hold that these insects *can* distinguish a pipe from a quack, the attempt to communicate seems doomed to failure. Try quacking, or piping, a sentence like 'We lost!' and you will see what I mean. The appropriate note of melancholy is altogether missing. As to any attempt to get through to a bee by means of its finely developed sense of touch – no.

There are reasons for thinking that even in the remoter areas of the West Country the bereaved sometimes doubted whether their sad spoken messages, piped or not, were fully understood within the hive. One has only to glance at the *Calender of Customs, Superstitions, Weather-lore, Popular Sayings, and Important Events Connected with the County of Somerset* (not, I realise, a book on everybody's shelves) to find that they employed a secondary means of communication quite independent of audible sounds or a sense of hearing. 'Turning the bees at a funeral,' writes the editor, Mr W.G. Willis Watson, 'was a custom peculiar to the West, and I am not sure it has yet (1920) died out. Of course, there is some danger in carrying out the operation. . . .' Indeed there is. As recently as 1790 the London *Argus* had a report, freely quoted by Mr Willis Watson, of the funeral of a farmer at Cullompton, in Devon, at which, just as the cortège was ready to move off, someone called out 'Turn the bees!' whereupon 'a servant, who had no knowledge of such a custom, instead of turning the hives round, lifted them up and laid them down on their sides!' The upshot proved conclusively that bees, however deaf, however insensitive to echoes, speaking trumpets, quacking, or any sound that Sir John Lubbock could devise, respond immediately to rotation through ninety degrees. These Cullompton bees attended the obsequies *en masse*. They attacked horses and riders, pursuing them tenaciously as they galloped off, and there ensued perhaps the briskest funeral ever seen in that quiet country town. 'General confusion took place,' observes my source mildly, 'attended with the loss of hats, wigs, etc.' The message, in short, had been received.

A final circumstance must be recorded. The bee in the kitchen, when I first saw it, was dashing about with all the agility of a McEnroe or a Connors, swooping from side to side of the arena, making swift sorties from dresser to windowpane and back, and stopping short with marvellous control within a fraction of an inch of this or that obstruction, varying its game the while with high lobs to the ceiling, where it seemed able, by the use of a top spin, to dart in any direction at will. A lively bee. Nastase himself at his best never whizzed about more athletically or buzzed with greater fury. Yet, returning within the hour, I found this selfsame bee inert and lifeless on the windowsill. It is my belief, whatever the Lubbocks and the von Frisches may say, that the shock of my news had been too much for it. It was, after all, a British bee.

Ancestral Voices

I suppose I qualified as Chairman of this Selection Board through a combination of too much curried lobster and a long evening's reading about human variation and the origins of man. It doesn't matter. There we were, surrounded by a roomful of candidates as hairy and beetle-browed as you could wish to see. One of them began to recommend himself, in what I took to be typically Pleistocene accents, before I had even got my bifocals on or my pencil properly squared off on top of my note pad.

CHAIRMAN: One moment, please. Allow me to introduce my fellow-assessors on the board. Mr Darwin, Dr Wallace, Sir Arthur Keith, Dr Leakey, Professor Dart, l'Abbé Breuil, Dr Stewart, Professor Dobzhansky, Eugene Dubois, Professor G.H.R. von Koenigswald, Professor Coon, Professor Asimov, and thirty-six other anthropologists, zoologists, palaeontologists and geochemists whose names I forget. Dr Huxley has been detained by a Bishop Wilberforce and sends his apologies.

A VOICE: His anthropapologies, surely?

CHAIRMAN: This is not a time for jesting. Will candidates who wish to speak begin by stating their names or species, preferably in italics? And one at a time, if you will be so good.

A VOICE: *Homo erectus* – once known as Peking Man. Which proves my point, I think. If, as I understand it, Mr Chairman, the business of your board is to determine the earliest True Man – though what, in that case, all these propliopithecoids and proconsuls are doing here beats me entirely, considering that some of them had hardly come down out of the trees, whereas I myself had no sooner been discovered in the Chou-kou-tien Caves when—

A VOICE: *Ramapithecus*. I am fourteen million years old, as dated by the potassium-argon method and vouched for by Professor E.L. Simons, of Yale, and I very much resent this slur from so-called *Homo erectus*, who can barely remember the Middle Ice Age, and, what is more, had cracked thigh bones when found *and* a hole in his skull through which the brains, such as they were, had been extracted, suggesting cannibalism. Speaking as I do on behalf of *Bramapithecus* and *Kenyapithecus wickeri*, both of whom, as you will know, sir, have been subsumed under my own genus by David R. Philbeam, working in conjunction with Professor Simons, I wish to state that we Lower Pliocene primates from India and East Africa—

HOMO ERECTUS: Never mind my cracked thigh bones. If *Ramapithecus* will take the trouble to read Mr Lewis Mumford's paper in *The American Scholar*, Vol. 36, he will see that the extraction of marrow in my day may have been part of a 'sacrificial, magico-religious ceremony', or, perhaps, used to help light a fire. And what about kidney transplants as practised by *Homo sapiens*? Even a pongid, I imagine, would hardly describe that as cannibalism in present company.

CHAIRMAN: Gentlemen, gentlemen! And ape-men, too, of course. Personal abuse, except as between members of the board, will get us nowhere. I must ask you to address all remarks to the Chair.

A VOICE: It's all this measuring of brainpans that I object to.

CHAIRMAN: Name, please?

VOICE: *Australopithecus* – when I last heard, that is. Though some say *Zinjanthropus boisei* (*laughter*), and dear old Leakey there used to call me *Homo habilis*.

Anyway, I'm tired of being written off, or down, as a six-hundred-cubic-centimetre skull. One is not a motor bicycle. It is not the volume that matters but the density of the contents, and what do all those grinning palaeontologists know about *that*? If a black hole in space can contain a billion times more—

AEGYPTOPITHECUS: Nobody doubts your density, old man.

AUSTRALOPITHECUS: I am obliged by the 'old man' – a term that no one would dream of applying to *Aegyptopithecus*, who reeks of the Late Oligocene. As a well-known tool user in the old days at Olduvai—

NEANDERTHAL MAN: Oh, I say, let us have no claims based on tool using, for pity's sake, or we shall have *Camarhynchus pallidus* piping up next!

CHAIRMAN: I'm not quite—Is there a *Camarhynchus pallidus* in the house?

NEANDERTHAL MAN: I am referring, as some of your zoological colleagues may know, to the woodpecker finch, which employs a cactus thorn to extract maggots from awkward crevices.

RAMAPITHECUS: Better look out for that skull of yours, *Homo erectus*.

NEANDERTHAL MAN: If, as I was saying, we are going to talk about tools, let us at least distinguish between tool *makers* and pitiful apes who occasionally bashed about with ready-made round stones, chipped or not. Even then, if anybody is going to stand up and say that the first toolmakers were the first men, why did it take them a million and a half years to turn out any worthwhile implements? The hallmark of Man, sir, is the ability to evolve rapidly. Now, a colleague of mine from the Shanidar Cave, in Iraq, had an arm amputated around forty-six thousand years ago – as I am sure Dr T. Dale Stewart, of the Smithsonian Institute, will agree – and survived. There's progress for you. Beetle-browed we may have been, and hairy (though I doubt whether all members of the board will fault us for that), but our arms were short, unlike those of some candidates I could name, and I should like to remind you all that the description of us as stunted, stooping, and shambling, given by M. Marcellin Boule as recently as 1911, has now been corrected by two eminent professors of anatomy, who diagnosed arthritis – a thoroughly human characteristic.

CHORUS OF HOMINIDS: Is that why you so soon became extinct?

AFRICANTHROPUS NJARASENSIS: Sofarash um consherned—

CHAIRMAN: Could you speak a little more distinctly?

GRIMALDI MAN: I don't think he can. One of your colleagues has got three-quarters of the lower half of his jaw.

CHAIRMAN: I see. Anybody else?

DRYOPITHECUS: I follow Hockett and Ascher, of Cornell. The vital attainment that eventually distinguished civilized man from the beasts was, as they rightly claim, the act of *carrying* – the ability to transport possessions, from twigs to credit cards, from one place to another. Now, I was a great carrier. Evidence may be lacking, but I must point out to the Chairman that even the most headstrong anthropologist would hesitate to deduce twig carrying from a couple of molars dug up in North-west India. You must take my word for it.

CRO-MAGNON MAN: This is becoming ridiculous. The time has come to put a stop to the chattering of these pitiful pongids, pithecoids, anthropoids, hominids, and ape-men of every kind, who try to better themselves on no sounder basis than an upper jaw or bits of an ankle bone mulled over by some palaeontologist with Miocene mud all over his boots. 'His jaw was roomy enough for a tongue to be used in speech' – that's Professor Berrill, of Swarthmore, chattering away in his turn about a fragment of *Homo habilis*. How does he know it wasn't roomy enough to eat two bananas at the same time? Are you aware, sir, that in the search for the origins of man, apart from the size of the skull, wear of teeth, descent from the trees, bipedalism, shape of the feet, use of weapons, speech, tools, carrying ability, genes, an opposable thumb, embryology, blood groups, fire, cooking, and ritual, anthropologists have adduced in evidence the closure of the orbit behind the eye, the ability to slaughter elephants, and a sense of humour? But the critical divergence of man from ape is to be found in no such trifle. It is the ability to reproduce (*loud laughter*) – to reproduce on the walls of caves or other suitable surfaces the veritable lineaments of the world about us upon which I base.... In short, it is as the first artist that I confidently claim to be the original representative of True Man.

CHAIRMAN: Thank you. No doubt Aurignacian Man will have something to say on that subject. We have also yet to hear, I note, from *Meganthropus palaeojavanicus, Homo modjokertensis, Paranthropus, Telanthropus*, Swanscombe Man, and, of course, *Gigantopithecus blacki*. Nor am I unaware that twenty or thirty members of the board have for some time been indicating their willingness to put in a word. As the hour is approaching the noon recess, I therefore suggest that we adjourn at this time and reconvene – shall we say – a thousand years from now.

A VERY SMALL LEMUR: By which time, I daresay, competition to claim prime responsibility for the human race may have sensibly declined.

The Last Redoubt

In a world of satire and abuse, charge and counter-charge, screamed invective, cries of 'Out pig!' and an increasing determination to dismiss fellow citizens not just as misguided, incompetent or wrongheaded but as charlatans, impostors, racialists, murderers, liberal intellectuals or floggers, there has remained one sequestered nook, one corner of kindness, one medium, damn it, where the bitter word is not thought to be normal currency, nor unveiled contempt to be the sign manual of integrity.

The local paper looks out from its eyrie in, or just off, the High Street of its pleasant market town and sees all around it a world of quite astounding excellence. Good works abound. Talks at Women's Institutes are uniformly interesting, 'most interesting' very often, and somebody does not hesitate to say so openly and to thank the speaker for her trouble in a few well-chosen words. The dead turn out to have been popular and respected. Bridget Flynn, of 19 Wellington Road, gained the top award for flutes in a competition open to the whole county. Congratulations on a wonderful year's work are showered about on fire brigades, postmen, guilds. Broccoli is plentiful and of good quality. So are visitors, cakes, whist drives, outings and plans for the improvement of shopping areas. People present things to worthy recipients, full face, on almost every page. It is true that a carping note is sometimes audible on the leader page, when the delay over the modernisation of a sewage plant has brought a momentary frown to the editor's forehead, but the criticism is measured, reasonable, and non-personal. The instant removal of the Borough Engineer is not demanded. You may search the paper's headlines in vain, too, for such angry catch-phrases as 'Dangerous Nonsense', and its gifted writers never ape the political weeklies with lofty references to the 'myth' of this and the 'myth' of that. Here at least people's cherished and lifelong beliefs and enthusiasms are not dismissed with scorn as childish fantasies.

Facts are faced, mind. Crime is boldly recorded, and the discovery of a bottle-top in a loaf of bread at West Popham is not blinked. The editor is not a man to sweep things under the carpet. But he has the courage also to face the good, the virtuous and the praiseworthy. When he comes across fourteen years of unstinted service to the Bagworthy Flower Show, he records it. It is his good fortune to have to chronicle week by week the doings of a community that is generally admitted to be practically faultless, whether in devotion to duty, organising ability ('the smooth efficiency we have come to expect,') the arts ('rendered her solo with professional aplomb,') vegetables ('a veritable headache for the judges,') or general downright niceness ('"Shall never forget your lovely town or its lovely people," declares Boston visitor') – and he feels no need to be ashamed of the task.

Yet, whoa! What is this?

'Miss— would probably have lost little had she simply read her part. Mr— would certainly have done better to read his.'

I do not desire to give further publicity to this disgraceful lapse on the part of my own local paper by repeating any more of it. It cuts clean across the traditions of country journalism. It is a worm i' the bud. Such language about the performance of a village dramatic society which (on the repeated evidence of the selfsame paper over the years) never fails to reach a standard that might well be the envy of the West End could deal an almost fatal blow to the self-confidence of every amateur actor between Cladbury and Thrupwell Regis. Young men and maidens from the farm and the boutique do not give up their spare time in order to be told they made a mess of it. What is the editor thinking of to let this critical nonsense – dangerous nonsense – smear the hitherto unsullied pages of our Gazette? Is he launching a campaign for fearless reporting and, if so, what is to become of that aura of triumphant good will in which we live and work? Where is this thing, so ill begun, to end? Will the Rural District Council, will the Rotary Club, will the Women's Institute itself be safe from abuse?

TEPID HIGH JINKS AT MINFORD

A smallish gathering at Minford W.I. heard Mrs Olive Rake stumble through an account of her recent visit to Italy. The President returned thanks when she sat down. First prize in the Decorated Potato competition went to Mrs Partridge for a really lamentable tuber, and tea was sloppily dispensed by the Misses Mary and Rachel Bung. Gossip followed.

The blood runs cold at the possibility of such liberties. We have the finest vegetables you ever saw round here, but what will become of them once this narking metropolitan attitude gets loose at the Flower Show? 'Little justification for the expression of smug satisfaction one saw on the faces of numerous exhibitors. Broad beans pitted and malformed.... Tomatoes a travesty.... As to potatoes, Miss String (1st Prize) would have been well advised to eat hers rather than show them. Mr Bisgood (Highly Commended) would not. Opening the Show with a charming record of forty-two consecutive clichés....'

There are plenty of failed Fleet Street men and ex-TV interviewers ready to come down and sprinkle their destructive bile over our genial villages, if that is what the editor wants. I could write the new-style leaders myself, with ease. 'The myth of Bulhampton's pre-eminence as the fairest and friendliest city in the West was finally exploded last Wednesday,' I should begin, 'when three Americans were overcharged in the Hat Market and a Mr Gregory from Birmingham lost his galoshes in the mud at the entrance to the Old Folk's Garden of Tranquillity. Bulhamptonians must learn to come to terms with reality. Quite apart from criminal negligence in the Public Library. . . .'

Bulhamptonians, however, need not worry. Bulhampton is, in fact, the fairest and friendliest city in the West and has the good fortune to be situated among the best vegetables, the finest actors, singers, talkers and potato decorators, the most respected citizens, living or recently dead, and the neatest tea-dispensers that perhaps even the West has ever seen. All the bridges make charming pictures, and there is no Hat Market. Truth will always triumph over bile.

Siskins under the Skin

A change has come over nature writing – nature novels, I should perhaps say – since I was a boy. In those days, the hero was likely to be a lynx or a puma which showed unmistakable signs from earliest cubhood of its coming overlordship of Baldneck Ridge, buffeting its playmates about with a will and surprising its proud parents by killing a brush turkey singlehanded before the first week was out. There was a good deal of blood in these stories; challenges were freely offered and accepted, manes bristled, hackles rose, claws rent and tore, and under the tingling stars a long-drawn menacing roar proclaimed to his waiting mate that old Moween, the black bear, was still supreme on the mountain. The animal hero enjoyed a certain anthropomorphic licence in this heady and exciting world (which generally, as I remember, seemed to be somewhere in Canada) and did not scorn an occasional recognisably human thought or emotion. A really tiptop bison might engage, before a decisive clash, in something pretty close to a soliloquy.

The nature books I pick up now are written in a quieter, less Homeric key. They aim to instruct rather than to paralyse. 'In the afternoon,' they are apt to begin, 'the mackerel turned south, seeking warmer waters, and browsed upon the rich herds of copepods and squids with which the waters of the continental shelf abounded.' Or they concern birds. 'On the third day, the wind freshened, scudding rain clouds blew up from the west, and heavy raindrops began to fall on a single specimen of dwarf-tufted centaury, which had been brought hither as a seed three years ago on the foot of a roving blackheaded gull and now, far from the sandy shores which are its normal habitat, gratefully raised its blunt, stalkless flower clusters to meet the shower. The siskins, feeding busily among the alders with their characteristic *clee-ip* and *shreeee* calls, were unaware, until it was almost too late, of the approach against the darkening sky of a raptor some fourteen inches in length, with whitish closely-barred underparts and the pale supercillary stripe of a female sparrow hawk. Hurtling forward on short, rounded wings. . . .'

Yes, well, I had better stop before I get carried away and start a full-scale spring migration. But I can tell you what happens, if you like. The siskins flee in panic. Two of them, becoming separated from the rest, mate in the course of a chapter handled fearlessly but without suggestive undertones, and the hen then builds a nest at the extremity of a conifer branch and lays five eggs in it. They are eaten by squirrels. She lays again, and the first nestling hatched, though not destined to be the strongest, bravest, and most intelligent siskin ever to become overlord of the Grampians, will yet be distinguished by a gray feather in its greenish-yellow wing bar, so that we shall be able to follow with ease its progress through adolescence to full birdhood. It will encounter, this little chap (whom we shall be careful, I hope, not to call 'Grayfeather'), many, many other inhabitants of the natural world as it goes about its business, and all of them will be described with care and accuracy. It will have innumerable narrow escapes from predators, guns, gins, tempest, and starvation, and when in due course it becomes a father we shall all be filled with a strong sense of the cycle of the seasons and the surge and rhythm of the life principle. But there will be no truckling with anthropomorphism, no indulgence in overt meditation. Siskins don't soliloquise.

The wide appeal enjoyed by this kind of nature novel is not hard to understand. Here we have a young couple

– siskins, badgers, raccoons, or what you will – whose simple wish is to eat, mate, have children, and keep alive. These are desires readily appreciated by most readers. The creatures will also, if they are migrant birds, experience from time to time an almost irresistible yearning to travel, or, if hedgehogs, to go to sleep for three or four months, and with these aims not too many human beings will be out of tune. Sympathy for the engaging pair is guaranteed from the start and, more significantly, is constantly quickened by the atmosphere of imminent, yet not oppressive, danger in which they lead their harmless, necessary lives. The actual flow of blood may be less Niagaran, the crunching of thigh bones a good deal less earsplitting than it used to be when Kaga, the wise old timber wolf, was on the prowl, but all the same this is no tame suburban world. It is nothing for a sandpiper, in any well-constructed nature novel, to be in immediate fear of death three times between leaving its nest on the sandpit and returning to it with some suitable mollusc. This keeps up the interest. So does the rich variety of characters among which the principals operate. A weasel pokes his pale nose out of the undergrowth, sniffs the air, and withdraws. Oyster-catchers far out on the mud flats set up a shrill crying and calling that may well presage danger for the young fledglings but in fact mean nothing. A purple hair-streak flits by and reindeer come down from the north in unprecedented numbers.

It is impossible to exaggerate the advantages in freedom, variety, and rapidity enjoyed by the nature novelist over his social or humanist colleague. You cannot, in an ordinary novel, successfully introduce a character who pokes his nose out-of-doors, sniffs the air, withdraws, and is never heard of again. If fifty women set up a shrill uproar in a field, it will not do simply to let the noise die down, register a change of wind, and leave it at that. The air of expectancy engendered must be justified in half a dozen tedious explanatory pages. If any reader – or writer, for that matter – doubts this elementary truth, he had better try to pack into a paragraph or two about people as much incident and interest as he would certainly be required to do if he were writing about siskins:

'Abandoning the now empty perambulator, the man and his mate made their way aimlessly northward for another forty or fifty miles, moving with strong alternate swings of their trousered legs and holding their heads characteristically a little withdrawn into their shoulders, as though to lessen the resistance to the keen wind that already had in its icy breath a touch of winter. Near Biggleswade, a burst of gunfire, recognised as inimical through the operation of those glandular mechanisms so often miscalled "instinctive" by less knowledgeable writers, made them swerve aside into the fields, and once the woman narrowly escaped barking her delicate shins on a solitary rear axle dropped long ago in a clump of nettles by some itinerant motorist. Hunger gnawed at their complicated digestive organs, and as the day waned, attracted by a small knot of their own kind in a crowd of some hundred others, they turned into a cafeteria, where they began in a desultory way to gather food.

'Squabbles were frequent on this packed feeding ground. Two cabdrivers tugged and pulled at a ham sandwich until it fell apart and was promptly snapped up by a watchful sanitary engineer. A marauding optometrist who had not fed for thirty-six hours caused a momentary panic by swooping suddenly upon a squawking Latvian waitress and carrying her off to a corner table where he leisurely tore her limb from limb. A party of two dozen pawnbrokers, rare visitors at this time of year, arrived with clamorous cries, their striped waistcoats and well-defined mustachial streaks showing them to be passage males.

'A sense of unease came upon the man's mate, and she left, drawn ever northward by an age-old mysterious urge. Reluctantly the man followed her, his blood warmed and thickened by the calories he had unknowingly ingested with his four slices of pizza. The sun set and rose. The wind blew yet more chilly from out of the north, and the man, tarrying, began to gather sticks and old sheets of newspaper, which he wove together into a kind of pyre, deftly tucking in odd corners and stray fragments of bark with his surprisingly nimble fingers. His mate watched him as he laboured and after a while brought him a small twig, which he accepted without the customary ceremonious bow and laid with the rest. Rain and sleet fell from a leaden sky, and the man lit the fire.

'It kindled, bringing warmth to their numbed members and lulling the pair into a half-sleep that night well have proved to be their last. A homicidal maniac, drawn thither by the flickering blaze. . . .'

It is apparent, is it not, that this kind of thing won't do for human beings? Only in the natural world is an author at liberty to beset his principal characters with perils, alarms, excursions, bereavements, meals, sex, ceremony, mysterious urges, and change of wind at the rate of six sensational episodes per page. It makes one wonder why more of the great writers don't write about nature, instead of tying themselves down to the cramped and uneventful world of men. The answer is, I suppose, that when writing about animals you have to know your subject.

A Contract with Cunard

1961

My Dear Cunard Steam-Ship Company, Ltd:

I am well aware that any kind of ticket, whether it be for leaving a hat in a cloakroom or flying to Japan, carries certain Conditions of Sale printed on the back, in full or in part, or implied or referred to, or drawn to the attention of the purchaser by notice or other means affixed or impaled on the wall of the office, bureau, cubbyhole, or any other place whatsoever where the ticket is, was, has been, or will be obtained. I also know that any purchaser who has the curiosity to examine such Conditions and the patience to wade right through a paralysing morass of tiny print will find that the person or persons who sold him his ticket have been at pains to rid themselves of almost all responsibility for his hat or his person, as the case may be, and have covered themselves against anything that he or they may or may not do in a series of disastrous contingencies to which the whole history of the world can scarcely afford a parallel.

It is also clear to me that in contracting to convey me and my baggage ('or provide transportation as specified herein', to use your own phrase) from Liverpool to New York you cannot be expected to undertake so arduous and even hazardous a task with the half dozen or so slipshod provisos thought adequate for the temporary custody of an overcoat at a theatre. The sea is an unstable element, indifferent to man's wishes, setting at nought his most careful contrivings, and I certainly do not propose to cavil at any of the 'liberties' you so rightly reserve on my ticket for yourselves, your ship, her master, your agents, and others, in a praiseworthy attempt to foresee and guard against the innumerable surprises and mischances of a voyage across the pitiless Atlantic. No man of sense and good will could object to Clause 3, for instance, of your Terms and Conditions, which begins (you will remember):

3. The ship shall have liberty to proceed with or without pilots, to tow and assist vessels in all situations, to be towed, to adjust compasses, to drydock with the passengers and their baggage on board, to carry cargo of all kinds, dangerous or otherwise, to comply with any orders or directions as to departure, arrival, routes, ports of call, stoppages, destination or otherwise, given by the government of any nation or department thereof or by any person acting or purporting to act with the authority of such government, or any department thereof, or by any committee or person having under the terms of the war risk insurance on the ship the right to give such orders or directions, and if by reason of and in compliance with such orders or directions anything is done or is not done the same shall not be deemed a deviation and compliance with the same shall be deemed a fulfilment of the contract voyage. . . .

By all means. Let the ship be towed and adjust compasses as necessary. Should I at any time during the voyage poke my head out of my porthole, attracted by an unfamiliar sound of hammering, and observe that we are hard and fast in a concrete container, shored up by vast baulks of timber, while men chip busily away at the barnacles on our hull, you will not find me at the head of a throng of passengers angrily complaining that this was not the purpose for which I and my baggage came on board. I shall fully understand that some person or committee or other had, in all probability, got us into this pickle, and I shall readily agree that whatever is done or not done, or wherever we are or are not (even if we are back in Liverpool again), the contract voyage has been fulfilled. I am not the kind of man lightly to bring a charge of deviationism against the master of a ship who, for all I know, may have cargo of all kinds, dangerous or otherwise, on board.

It is not, I see, altogether unlikely that we *shall* be back in Liverpool again. Clause 3 continues (I need hardly remind you):

. . . to proceed by any course or route whatsoever although in a contrary direction to or out of or beyond the direct or geographical or customary or advertised route to the port of destination once or oftener in any order, backwards or forwards, without notice to passengers, and for any such purpose to call and/or remain or omit to call and/or remain at any port or ports, place or places whatsoever, to put back or into any port at the discretion of the master and to deviate from the direct and customary course, and to carry the passengers and their baggage back to the port of embarkation or to any port or place whether beyond the port of destination or not, and to make any delay whatsoever at, or in sailing from, the port of embarkation or any such port or place as aforesaid....

and to all of this, let me say at once, I give my hearty consent. I quite see that circumstances might arise in which the master of your ship might wish to sail out of or beyond or in a contrary direction to the port of destination, and might be compelled to shuttle backwards and forwards, once or oftener, in any order and for any number of years whatsoever without calling or omitting to call at any port or place, with or without pilots, whether such ports or places were or were not behind, in front of, or beyond any destination whatsoever from which any ship of yours had previously deviated. It is true that the expression 'backwards or forwards' reads a little oddly in a context where one might have expected 'ahead or astern', but in general I would no sooner dream of contesting the propriety and necessity of Clause 3, in whole or in part, with or without commas, than I would question the wisdom of Clause 19 ('Any person carried under this ticket hereby assumes all risk of war and warlike operations....'), or of that other bit that warns me not to try to hold you liable for injury or delay to myself or my baggage 'arising from dangers of the sea or other navigable waters, Acts of God or public enemies, barratry of master or crew' – do you get much of that, I wonder? – 'seizure under legal process, saving or attempting to save life or property at sea or from any deviation,' etc, etc.

No. In all these matters I accept you as the experts, and I do not doubt that your twenty-two Terms and Conditions are the result of bitter experience – of countless occasions on which passengers have made a fuss simply because they have been carried into or out of or beyond, or backwards and forwards in any order, or because of some trivial piece of barratry, or because anything whatsoever has been done or not done. My complaint, such as it is, is purely on a matter of presentation, about which I know at least as much as you.

All of your Conditions are set out in 8-point type, in which I have reproduced sections of them above. It is, as anyone can see, a perfectly legible type size. But you seem not to be aware of the old printer's rule that lays down that 'for easy reading'

> 8-point type should not be set wider than four inches
> 10-point type should not be set wider than five inches
> 12-point type should not be set wider than six inches

– the reason being, of course, that there is a width beyond which the eye cannot readily follow printing from line to line.

The column of Conditions (Nos. 1–3) on the front of my ticket is just under six inches wide, which means that the passenger, in attempting to discover what he has let himself in for, runs a grave risk of reading the same line several times over, skipping a line (which may contain upwards of twenty-five words about doing or not doing anything whatsoever), and in general proceeding by a course or route contrary to or out of or beyond the direct and customary manner of reading, once or oftener in any order, backwards or forwards. This is a risk that I am *not* prepared to accept, and one, moreover, that is nowhere covered by your Conditions.

Whether you prefer to narrow your column to four inches or to set your Conditions in 12-point, as the printer's rule appears to require, is for you to decide. The latter would insure maximum legibility; here, for your convenience, is a specimen of 12-point:

BARRATRY OF MASTER OR CREW

I must warn you, however, that this resetting will increase the size of your ticket from its present dimensions of seventeen inches wide by ten and an eighth inches long to something like seventeen inches by twenty, which might prove unwieldy in a high wind.

A more serious problem arises when we turn to the back of the ticket, where Clauses 4–22 are set, you will notice, at a column width of no less than ten inches – possibly a world record for 8-point. The printer's rule does not, so far as I know, extend to type sizes suitable for lines of such interminable length, but by a process of extrapolation we arrive at a minimum of 20-point, and I am not sure that you would care either for the hint of overemphasis in a phrase like

WARLIKE OPERATIONS

or for the formidable acreage of ticket involved. You may decide, on reflection, to cut down the number of Conditions.

And where, as a matter of interest, do you get that hyphen in 'Steam-Ship Company'?

The Aisle is Full of Noises

1975

The vicar is now kneeling on a hassock in the central aisle, to lead us in our special prayers this Sunday morning. The earlier, more canonical prayers (the Collects, in fact) he delivers from his own pew up in the chancel, but he always descends for this second selection. He feels, I dare say, that he wants to be with us and of us at this stage, less sacerdotal – even though the soles of his shoes become so clearly visible from the rearward pews. When I was a boy, an inch of workaday toecap protruding from the hem of a cassock made me uneasy; there was a sense of let-down, of the kind you get when some amateur Othello has failed to carry the blacking far enough up his arms. But I cannot pretend to be distracted now even by a glimpse of purple sock. It is inevitable, as the years roll on, that much of the mystique departs from a vicar who regularly bespeaks a few dozen of one's broccoli plants every June and sometimes proffers a bag of horse-manure in exchange. The unease that troubles me during these aisle prayers has deeper roots.

The Vicar begins, as usual, by suggesting that we address ourselves to the disturbed areas of the world. 'Let us pray,' he says, 'that peace may return to the world and that good will and wise counsels may prevail.'

This is within my compass. I do not feel, as I shift my spectacle case along the pew ledge to make way for my left elbow and rest my forehead on my folded hands, that there is anything innately absurd in giving a silent 'Aye' to this proposition. Most of mankind, to whomever or whatever they pray, would find smal difficulty in joining in a general wish for peace rather than war, friendliness rather than hatred, wisdom in preference to folly and, as the Vicar puts it, 'mutual understanding and harmony among the nations.'

But the Vicar has not finished with the subject. 'Let us pray,' he adds, 'for the distressed peoples of South-East Asia.' He asks for concord between Jew and Arab. He prays for Northern Ireland and Chile. He invites our attention to Cyprus. He sought, until our prayers were answered, divine intervention in the Cod War, which he called 'the discontents obtaining between ourselves and Iceland'. He has a passion for itemising. It is not enough for him that we should intercede 'for those in distress of mind, body or estate, wherever they may be'; he seems to have no faith in blanket supplications but must forever be pointing the finger at this disaster or that centre of unrest, whatever the difficulties of pronunciation involved. He is on to an earthquake like a terrier after a rat. Flood and accident, fire, shipwreck and riot stream from his lips with the facility of an Excluding Clause in an Insurance Policy. He clearly listens to the radio at breakfast, and at Matins on Sunday mornings it is often from him (for our newspapers arrive latish in this small village) that we first hear of a typhoon in the China Seas or a collapsed bridge in Uruguay. 'I had it straight from the hassock', churchgoers have been heard to say to their less regular neighbours; nor would any of us be greatly surprised if some member of the Vicar's family were to come hurrying up the aisle with a Stop Press item that seemed to call for his, and our, intervention.

Against this *catalogue raisonné* of current misfortunes my mind rebels. I am unable to conceive of a Being who, on top of a general requirement to promote harmony and relieve distress throughout the globe, needs to have his benevolence specifically directed to a whole series of regions and map references; and if He does, am I to suppose that a failure to mention Argentine or the Near East, here in this elderly congregation of thirty or so men and women, would actually reduce the chances in those parts of a happy issue out of all their afflictions? I am also aware that vicars in many other parishes hereabouts, to stray no further afield, are at this very moment interceding for or against South Africa, volcanoes and industrial unrest. If half-a-dozen of them remember Chile, is it to be believed that a momentary forgetfulness on our own Vicar's part, still less on mine, will tip the balance? The thing cannot surely be settled on an actuarial basis.

Looking right-handed across the aisle I see that Miss Tankery is in a posture of really dedicated prayer, and the same, in his more hunched way, could be said of old Rybarts two pews in front of me. Obviously, while my own thoughts have been temporarily diverted to the probable subjects of devotion at Huish Episcopi and Stogumber, others in the congregation here have not neglected whatever storm-centre the Vicar is concerned with now. No neglect of mine ought, it seems to me, to negative or even diminish the effect of Mrs Brinton's palpable concentration on Bangladesh, or, it may be, Mozambique. Humility, an acknowledged Christian virtue, must lie, I am glad to think, at the root of my firm conviction that no intervention or non-intervention of mine is going to determine the issue in any quarter of the globe. Soon, with any luck, I shall have elevated my lack of attention into a positive act of grace.

However, the Vicar has now brought us nearer home. He is praying for our Government and for all those who exercise authority and influence over the minds of men, that they may be guided and strengthened in all their endeavours; and for the time being I am with him again. This is the kind of prayer that needs all the support it can get, as an objective observer might deduce from the fact that I have now pressed my fingertips together to form an inverted V and am resting the bridge of my nose against the apex. But almost at once the Vicar lapses again from the general to the particular. He does not mention the members of the Cabinet by name, but he certainly departmentalises. Education, Agriculture and Health ('All doctors and nurses, and those who voluntarily minister to the sick') are today's specialities; also the Press and, indeed, 'all who seek to guide opinion by their writings or through broadcasting, that they may strive always for the advancement of thy Kingdom.' I cannot bring myself to supplicate for the media, having perhaps a clearer picture of the workings of a Fleet Street office than the Vicar, nor (for he is now constricting still further the radius of his intercessions) am I inclined to put in a helpful word for the deliberations of our County Council. The fact is that I am getting cramp up the back of my right thigh, and first things must come first.

Yet here is a curious thing. We have now, in our accustomed centripetal course, begun to pray for our homes, our village and, in particular, for Jimmy Harwood ('broken leg'), Mrs Trewint ('stricken with pleurisy') and Colonel Sharpe ('recuperating in hospital'). Here, in the naming of individuals, is the very ultimate in intercessional breakdowns, yet I do not at all resent this fine splitting of prayers nor wish to dissociate myself from these highly localised proceedings. On the contrary, crouching low over my pew rail at the mention of Mrs Trewint, with hands pressed firmly over my eyes, I fall no whit behind even old Rybarts in the fervour of my concentration. I by no means despair of speeding her recovery, nor of hastening the return home of Colonel Sharpe.

Where is my humility now? And if I think I can do a good turn for the Colonel, why should I doubt my efficacy in the matter of persecutions in Russia or cholera in the Far East? Well, of course, one can argue that if the Colonel's case is to be put forward anywhere it must be here. Small chance of his name cropping up at Huish Episcopi this morning. But then they, like us, will have done what they can for him already in their general prayers for the sick. One is piling Pelion on Ossa, in a way. Besides, it is not more than two and a half minutes by my watch since we were extending a helping hand to all doctors and nurses – not excluding those who have the Colonel in their charge. Would it not show more confidence in them (to go no higher) if we left it at that?

The Vicar is at last on his feet, which are now mercifully obscured. It is not, as I have said, that their appearance as such any longer disenchants me with his office, but one can have too much of anything. The possibility of making a *mot* about the Feast of All Soles, which has for too long now been added to my other distractions, shows that I have not altogether put away childish things. However,

'Let us join,' the Vicar is suggesting, 'in singing Hymn Number 43 "For All the Saints, who from their labours rest".'

By all means. My right leg is giving me agony.

I suppose, if I were to lay before the Vicar my doubts about the propriety of praying in detail for what we have already covered in general, he would tell me that I fail to comprehend the real nature of prayer. He would advise me to study the works of Sts Augustine and Athanasius, and might offer to lend me helpful books by such more recent authorities as Butler and Weatherhead and Bounds. The difficulty with clergymen is that they take things so seriously. 'We must have a good talk about it all one day.' I hear him saying.

On the other hand, he might be in one of his brisker moods, and say no more than 'All *you* want, of course, is to feel that you have done your best for the world in five minutes flat, so that you can be home a quarter of an hour earlier for your pre-lunch gin-and-tonic.' I should not very much care for that either. On the whole it will be best, I think, to let him get on with his praying in the way that suits him, and try to concentrate more on my own feet of clay and less on his. It will be a comfort, if I am carried from his church one Sunday morning with some kind of intercrural seizure, to remember that I shall be providing one more bit of grist for his exceedingly small-grinding mill.

Rabelaisian Conclusion

Ward B, which is in the Surgical Block, faces Ward Q, in the Medical Block, across a courtyard wide enough to contain, in visiting hours, a very fine selection of Zephyrs, Minis, Jaguars, Cortinas and other makes. Ward Q is, I should guess, for chest cases; at any rate its outward wall consists almost entirely of glass, which may or may not admit beneficial rays but certainly exposes the inmates to view as mercilessly as a goldfish bowl.

The man in blue striped pyjamas who occupied the cubicle in Ward Q immediately opposite mine in Ward B was not, I judged, seriously ill. He was always wide awake, reading and smoking his first cigarette, by the time his post-temperature early tea came round – and that, in hospital, is early enough. Like me, he spent a fair proportion of the day out of bed, washed standing up at his basin, and regularly performed exercises, of a Swedish kind, before breakfast. Seen through glass at a distance of perhaps fifty yards his expression appeared to me to be equable, even amiable, and I was glad to see that, though short on visitors and fruit, he got at least one letter most mornings. When a parcel came for him, about my fourth day, he toyed with it, shook it against his ear to see whether it rattled, fiddled with the knots, and generally saved it up and put off the great moment in a way that affected me strongly. It was bad luck that a nurse came in to change my dressing before he had got beyond the stage of poking a tentative finger through the brown paper; but I am pretty sure the plum-coloured pullover he had on at lunchtime was new.

For the best part of a week, off and on, I eyed this

man: not inquisitively, you understand, but rather in a spirit of companionship. Here we both were, immured for a while, cut off from the world in our respective cells, and just as prisoners feel the need to tap out messages to one another on walls and water-pipes, so there grew upon me a desire to communicate, to exchange some sort of greeting, with this fellow in misfortune. Or, if 'desire' is too strong a word, I at least began to feel that it was stand-offish not to. So, on the sixth day, I waved.

Nothing occurred immediately to show what a capital mistake this was. The man in Q waved back, and that was that. The day rolled on its endless course, and each of us pursued our several ways. He continued, as ever, to read a single newspaper, patiently, interminably, hour after hour. I, in my fretful way, dipped into book after book and proved yet again that only in sickness has one the clarity of vision to see novels as they really are – the futile chronicles of men and women who never were, agonising over events that never happened. The salute, nevertheless, had been exchanged. We had done the civil thing.

Next morning it was of course unthinkable that we should fail to pass the time of day. But now a single wave seemed somehow a little cursory, and it occurred to me, after giving it, to point a finger upwards at the sky, which was charged with a November gloom, and then turn my thumb down in a gesture of condemnation. *Not* a very nice day. The man in Q replied, with a rather adroit opening of an imaginary umbrella, that it was going to rain. I agreed, adding by means of an exaggerated shrug in the Continental manner that it made little difference to the likes of *us*. He, too, turned the palms of his hands upwards, and there the conversation ended. Tomorrow, I remember thinking, I must ask him how he is getting on.

My belief is that the man in Q has a rather pessimistic

nature. He can touch his toes twelve times running to my certain knowledge, which is hardly an indication of any deep-seated malady; yet when I stabbed a finger in his direction the following morning, tapped my chest, coughed once or twice, and then raised my thumb in the air in an OK gesture, accompanied by a sort of interrogative outward semi-circle with the other hand, he gave only a very *comme ci, comme ça* account of himself, ending with a display of his wrist watch and a final stretching out of the arms, like a man boasting of a fish. Naturally these pulmonary complaints take time. 'Patience!' I wanted to tell him, and looked about for a monument to sit on, but finding none that I cared to use began to go through the motions of an old lady setting out cards, which plainly worried him. 'Forget it,' I signalled after a while, using the wash-out gesture, and soon afterwards the arrival of his breakfast put a stop to conversation for the day. But he could not seem to get the thing out of his head. I watched him lathering up for a shave later on and he was patently trying, with his free hand, to make sense of my dealing-out motions by attempting to repeat them; but he had missed that tell-tale flick of the wrist that inverts the cards as they are set down and was substituting a sideways twist of the fingers, so that as far as I could see he was either turning on a row of taps or perhaps unscrewing the stoppers of a car battery. What on earth did the man suppose I could have meant by that?

Overnight I worked out a rather ingenious inquiry about what the food was like over in Ward Q, but I had hardly begun the preliminary knife and fork action before he interrupted me with a pantomime of extra-ordinary complexity. First he took a tube of toothpaste and pressed the nozzle against his upper arm, then he flopped down on his bed and appeared to go to sleep. Rising up again he tied a handkerchief over his mouth, stropped what may have been a fountain pen or a toothbrush on a towel, arranged two pillows lengthwise on the bed and, bending over, drew the implement with some savagery right across the middle of the upper one. By the time he had got to the point of threading an imaginary needle I had had enough of it and I nodded my head six times in rapid succession, following this up with a rather curt OK sign.

He was, I suppose, within his rights in inquiring whether I had had surgical treatment, but to probe the matter further seemed to me downright impertinence. That, however, is what he did. The man's curiosity exceeded all bounds. Using his own body for demonstration purposes, he sawed off a finger and then a foot, performed a tracheotomy, trepanned himself rather clumsily, took out his appendix, made an inexplicable incision in his left calf – and after each manoeuvre stared across at me in a palpably interrogative way. I am just not prepared to discuss my operations with strangers at a distance of fifty yards. Courteous inquiries are one thing, but this was simply the morbid relish of the parish pump. I determined, with four or five days in Ward B still ahead of me, to put a stop to the acquaintance once and for all. Calling in aid all the resources of a cultured mind, wide reading, and a retentive memory, I stepped right up to my window and made with considerable emphasis the sign with which Panurge 'put to a non-plus the Englishman that argued by signs'.

'Why, Mr *Ellis*!' said the ward sister, entering on her morning round. 'Are you all right?'

Shall We, for God's Sake, Join the Ladies?

'The wines of Pomerol,' my host was saying, 'are on the whole less severe, a little softer, surely, than those from the other side of the Garonne?'

'Yes. Oh, yes,' one of my fellow-guests agreed. 'Though they lack, of course, the finesse of some of the finest growths of the Medoc. I recall a Margaux, a Château Rausan-Segla, actually, which had undertones . . . .'

The talk rolled over me. Full-bodied, robust, gentle, big, bold, light, fruity, and generous, of full bouquet, crisp, delicate, round, well balanced – the words glanced and glimmered in the mellow light, bounced like bubbles from mouth to mouth off the satin mahogany. I untwined my fingers from the stem of my glass, thinking them knobbly and not of the first growth. What exactly did 'well balanced' imply? Would it be possible, taking advantage of a brief nostalgic hush produced by the mention of Trockenbeerenauslese, to say with conviction that the wines of the Rheingau lacked equilibrium? It would not. The conversation had already moved on.

'Was it not a character in *The Egoist* who remarked that "Port is the Homeric hexameter, Burgundy the Pindaric dithyramb"?'

Soft candlelight, cultured minds, and the champagne, the Louis Roederer – nay, the very Chateau d'Yquem – of conversation, weaving connoisseurship in wine and literature together into a gently glowing tapestry . . .

who could ask for more? I sought refuge in a private train of thought started by the name of Homer. Homer's heroes indulged in a goblet from time to time, but I could not recall that they ever talked much about the experience. As for Pindar, the only verdict of his that came readily to mind was his notorious 'Water is best'. Was it possible that the Greeks, in addition to their other manifold and widely acknowledged excellencies, were not wine bores? Not even in the 'Symposium'. . . .

'There is an afterthought,' the man on my left was saying, 'a kind of delayed piquancy that you don't get in the wines of the Loire.'

'Sancerre but not *sans reproche*?' my host inquired, with a downward glance at his fingernails.

No Greek would ever have permitted himself to mistake balderdash for civilised conversation. The Greeks were fond of wine and took a great deal of trouble over its manufacture. I know this because not long ago, when looking up the Vestal Virgins (in Dr William Smith's *A Dictionary of Greek and Roman Antiquities*) I got sidetracked on 'Vinum' and emerged, twenty minutes later, with enough confused information to paralyse any dinner table for seven courses. The Greeks liked direct talk no less than they liked wine. They esteemed the Chian above all others, and said so. Next to it they inclined to rank Thasian and Lesbian, though some maintained that the Clazomenian knew no peer. But they never, to the best of my knowledge, declared that Thasian was robust and full-bodied but scarcely so generous as some of the finer Samian *crus*. They hadn't the culture for it.

'The processes used in winemaking in the Aegean in classical times,' I said at large – but they were talking about a 1955 Clos Vougeot, and when a momentary lull occurred I did not care to begin again. There are some openings that cannot be repeated, except after a longish interval, without sounding dangerously second-hand.

The processes were interesting, all the same. The Greeks, I recalled, used to ferment the juices of the grape in large earthenware jars, or pithoi, which had been well lined with pitch, sprinkled with sea water, fumigated with aromatic plants, and then half buried in the ground. When fermentation subsided and the worst of the scum had bubbled out, they rubbed the upper part of the interior of the pithoi with defrutum, saffron, old pitch, mastic, and fir cones, sealed her up, and stood clear. About once a month thereafter, they took the lid off again to air and cool the contents, and to add one or more of the many conditioners, emollients, flavourers, bouquet-lenders, and stimulants known to the ancients, of which only turpentine and –

'As noble a Gruaud-Larose,' I heard dimly through the curtain of my private thoughts, 'as was ever bottled at the Chateau.'

– resin, burnt marble, spices, raisins, goat's milk, and parched salt came off-hand to memory. They would also plunge blazing pine torches or red-hot irons into the savoury brew, but these were withdrawn again before the lid, well rubbed with fir cones, was replaced for another month.

This process went on until the wine was ready to be drawn off into the amphora, a handy nine-gallon affair (now found mainly at the bottom of the Mediterranean), which was stoppered with a plug of wood smeared with pitch or gypsum. Here it remained to mature, undisturbed except perhaps for the addition of a little more resin, a cedar cone or two, a drop of ungent, to suit the individual purchaser. Nothing now remained to be done before drinking but to clarify the wine with the yolk of pigeons' eggs, strain it into a bowl, mix with water, honey, and perhaps cheese (Circe's recipe) to taste, and invite the guests to try a sip. After that, an old Greek might have been forgiven, I think, if he had made rather a business of sniffing the aroma and rolling a tentative sip around the tongue before pronouncing it—

'A piquant wine,' somebody was asserting over my bowed head, 'of exceptionally full body.'

All right, then – before pronouncing it a piquant wine of exceptionally full body. But the old Greeks did nothing of the kind. Even in the 'Symposium' (which is, I suppose, the *locus classicus* for wine and talk in ancient Athens), there is practically no comment on the refreshments provided by host Agathon, beyond the fact that they gave Aristophanes hiccups and that only Socrates was still awake at dawn. This is especially praiseworthy because, being blessed with wines so various and enterprising in their ingredients, the ancients could have discussed them in direct and factual terms. They had no need to take refuge in the kind of nebulous driftwood about rotundity that my host was now casting upon the waters. They could have talked *sense* about wine:

ARISTODEMUS: I like this, Agathon. A nice tarry wine, thoroughly well balanced at the pithos stage. Not too much turps.

AGATHON: You don't think a pinch more burnt marble would have—

ERYXIMACHUS: No, no. It must be sparingly added, even when it comes from a quarry of the first grain – as, of course, has this. Pentelican, wouldn't you say? It burns more evenly than the Parian.

PAUSANIAS: I don't pretend to be an expert, but surely this must be. . . . No, don't tell me; the parched salt had me foxed for a moment. Yes. It's a Thasian! The wines of Thasos are on the whole less – how shall I put it? They taste less of red-hot irons than those from Lesbos or Clazomenae. But what does Socrates say? Come, Socrates. Tell us what you think of Agathon's wine.

SOCRATES: Very well, Pausanias. Do you agree that goat's milk is Good?

PAUSANIAS: Certainly it is.

SOCRATES: Is it, then, the goat or the milk that attains to excellence in the highest degree?

PAUSANIAS: You are trying to trip me up, Socrates. My answer is that both are of equal merit.

SOCRATES: Do the makers of wine, then, put the goat into the pithos, or is it not rather the milk only that —

ALCIBIADES: Spare us the Method tonight, Socrates. Just answer the question.

SOCRATES: Alcibiades has forgotten that, as men put pigeons' eggs into wine to clarify it, so in discourse—

AGATHON: I am sorry if they were not quite fresh, Socrates.

At this point in my private reflections, a silence fell on the company, and I took advantage of it to remark that the processes used in winemaking in the Aegean in classical times were not without interest. They used to ferment the must, I explained, in large earthenware jars, or pithoi, which had been previously well lined with pitch, sprinkled with sea water, and fumigated with aromatic plants. When fermentation subsided and the worst of the scum had bubbled out—

But connoisseurs are not interested in facts. 'Shall we?' my host suggested, in a voice as crisp as a Budesheimer Scharlachberg Steinkautweg Riesling '59.

A Cornish Wall

The beauty of a Cornish wall, of this Cornish wall at any rate, is its solidity. You can haul yourself up and over it at any point without fear of that sudden dislodgement so disconcerting to wall clamberers in limestone districts. It is wide, coheres by its own weight, and when it has reached the required height stops; no vertically set upper course, in the Cotswold manner, was thought necessary by its maker, still less is it topped by some fancy coping, drip-course or other concreted elaboration. It has beauty of colour, too, since lichens, mosses, thyme, stonecrop and a multitude of other undemanding guests have lodged themselves in its minute interstices and along its broad top, splashing and mottling its basic grey with purples, olives, umbers, chromes and here and there a brilliant streak of red.

I have been reading Dorothy Wordsworth's *Journals* and could, if I had her gift of observation and shorthand descriptive genius, immortalise this wall against which my back is resting in a couple of verbless sentences. 'The sea like a basin full to the margin,' she wrote; 'the dark fresh-ploughed fields; the turnips of a lively rough green. Returned through the wood.' A girl capable of transmuting a commonplace word like green by the addition of those two epithets would somehow have bathed my olives and umbers in the sunlight and sea air of this flawless September day. I cannot follow her. The fern that hangs so patiently within inches of my right eye refuses to disclose its secret. So it is fortunate that I am not concerned with this wall as raw material for some favourite poet. It is unlikely that a Coleridge will look over my shoulder as I make my jottings. I am at liberty to abandon the search for words beyond my compass and concentrate on the astonishing fact that my name has just been spoken on the further side of the barrier.

That, and a little more. 'Some sort of retired lecturer, by the look of him,' the man had said, before he passed out of earshot, and faintly in reply the woman's voice hazarded what sounded like 'Fringe BBC?'

Fringe BBC! It has never been clear to me just what I should prefer to be taken to be by other people in a hotel. A great surgeon? An ambassador resting between posts? Sir Mortimer Wheeler recovering from an attack of alopecia? What is certain is that I have never desired to be dismissed as 'fringe BBC', whatever the disgusting term may imply. It was not this, however, that darkened the sun for me and took all the chromes and umbers out of the wall. There came back to me a much more damaging phrase, employed by the woman before my name was mentioned and therefore only in retrospect arresting. 'Man with a bit of cornflake stuck to his lower lip,' she had said, and at once her husband – assuming the monstrous alliance to have been legalised – responded with his identification. He is the kind of man, I dare say, who scans the hotel register at hourly intervals, linking new names with new faces and afterwards, in company with the small-minded consort he so richly deserves, allotting them erroneous careers, in insufferably patronising tones.

Anyone can get a bit of cornflake momentarily adhering to his lip. It is the milk. Nice people at adjoining tables avert their eyes when these trivial mishaps occur. They do not nudge each other and point with their spoons and say 'Do look! There's a man over there with a bit of cornflake stuck to his lower lip. We must mull him over during our afternoon stroll to the cliff.'

How *long* was it there, for the Lord's sake? Not more than a second or two probably, or I should have noticed. Passing an exploratory hand over my mouth and chin I can be pretty certain it isn't there now at any rate. Well, naturally the morning bathe. . . . So that at the lunch table I must have been trim enough, though no doubt that abominable pair were eagerly watching to see whether a fragment of cabbage or some morsel of that crumbling Cheshire lodged itself – Tuh! The whole thing is too petty for words. In this warm and slightly scented air, a man with his back to a lichened wall, plenty of tobacco, and a fern gently caressing his right ear should be able to concentrate his whole mind on the beauty of the Cornish coastscape. The withered thrift; the stubble of a rough dead ochre; the sea, like a basin full of turnips.

Dorothy Wordsworth never had a cornflake stuck to her lower lip. Or, if she did, she made no note of it for Coleridge's benefit. What was that thing she wrote, though after a walk to Nether Stowey? 'One only leaf upon the top of a tree – the sole remaining leaf – danced round and round like a rag blown by the wind.' Was that how it looked in my case, to an ill-natured observer?

The one crisp flake, the last of its clan,
That dances as often as dance it can,
Hanging so light, and hanging so free
On the bottom lip of a retired lecturer,
who could perhaps be written off
instead as 'fringe BBC'

I must be careful not to let this silly trifle prey on my mind. One does not want to become known as the man who is for ever dabbing at his face with a napkin. And then again, having no faintest idea what that impertinent pair look like, am I to spend the rest of the holiday listening for intonations and hating everyone in the hotel meanwhile? There is a clump of close-growing vegetation away to my left that deserves a sensitive observer's contemplation. Could its particular shade of blue-green be described as spiky? Overcast? Demure?

They are coming back. On my side of the wall! Surely, if they have any sense of shame and their memories are not completely atrophied, a dull and ugly flush will mantle their cheeks when they come abreast? It does not. On the contrary, they stop and with the utmost affability pass the time of day. What lovely weather! Am I staying long? And where? Oh yes. They themselves are at the other place, further up the hill. . . .

'In that case. . . .' I begin, but decide, wisely I think, to leave it. I do not see, unless they are unusually interested in coincidences, that it will excite them to know that a fellow-guest of theirs, a rather sloppy eater with, I should guess, a desiccated and pseudo-artistic cast of countenance, bears the same surname as I. They express the hope, before they move off, that we may perhaps meet in the sea; and I share it. A nice couple.

The sea, blue and sparkling; the sky milky but not iridescent; the wall of a vivacious ochreous hue. Returned along the top of it, humming.

For a Gentleman of Fortune

1961

An advertisement for a domestic escalator (unused) in the Personal columns of the London *Times* would not in the ordinary way have held my attention. But it happened to coincide with a phase of pondering on the wisest uses of enormous wealth, which in turn had been triggered off by the appearance of the sad face of Mr J. Paul Getty on my television screen, and seemed, within limits, apt. Unaided, I have never had much success at imagining the kind of luxuries I should buy were I a man of super-abundant means. An essentially middle-income and suburban mind cannot lift itself at will out of the rut of bigger and better cars, innumerable shirts, a yacht equipped with quantities of Swedish glass in cabinets behind sliding doors that never stick. Domestic escalators strike me as being in quite a different bracket, with that little extra something that distinguishes one's property from all the others on millionaires' row. Or am I being naïve again? I never enter the houses of people with much above a hundred thousand a year, and it may well be that domestic escalators are a regular fitting in the residences of the really well-to-do. Mr Getty perhaps has half a dozen, on which he and his guests pass and repass each other at speeds determined by a gentle pressure on the handrail. Still, I ask myself, are they *carpeted*? There is no suggestion that the apparatus offered in the *Times* advertisement is other than the ordinary bare metallic affair, but one can always go a little further than the man next door, given resolution and the necessary means. 'The treads must be upholstered throughout in triple-pile Axminster,' I should tell Otis or Westinghouse, or whoever sees to these things. 'The carpeting must disappear at the top and come round again, unsoiled, at the bottom – or vice versa, naturally, on downward trips. Don't argue the matter. The difficulties will argue for themselves.'

No sooner have I written the words than the old creeping fear of being outdone by reality comes upon me. Is it possible that all this is old hat, that in fact an *un*carpeted escalator in Mr Getty's home would start a rumour that he was short of cash, and lead to something of a panic on the Stock Exchange? Let me withdraw that card and substitute another in which I have much more confidence.

After Mr Getty's television appearance and the *Times* advertisement ('any reasonable offer'), it was no surprise to me on picking up a copy of Gilbert White's *Natural History of Selborne* to come at once upon a passage beginning 'Should any gentleman of fortune think an echo in his park or outlet a pleasing incident, he might build one at little or no expense. For whenever he had occasion for a new barn, stable, dog-kennel, or the like structure, it would be only needful to erect this building on the gentle declivity of a hill, with a like rising opposite to it, at a few hundred yards distance; and perhaps success might be the easier insured could some canal, lake or stream intervene. From a seat at the *centrum phonicum* he and his friends might amuse themselves sometimes of an evening with the prattle of this loquacious nymph. . . .'

I think we are on to something here. Natural echoes are nothing out of the way and can be met with on the properties of persons of quite moderate means. Some of them have remarkable powers; I have read of a castle near Milan which has (or had) one reputed to echo the report of a pistol sixty times. A built-in echo is an altogether different kettle of fish. A man can be proud of an echo put in to his own specification, even if it be only a simple little thing of the kind envisaged by Gilbert

White. And I see no reason why it should be. If I had no more than a third of Mr Getty's millions, I should aim at something a bit more ambitious in my outlet. One need never be dull after dinner with a private echo that goes one better than the pride of Lombardy. Just let me sit at the *centrum phonicum* on a fine summer evening listening to my cry of 'Domestic escalators!' come back to me sixty-one times and I believe I should feel that the struggle had not been entirely in vain. 'Would you mind,' my friends would surely say as the clamour at last died down, 'letting me have the address of your echo man?' These are the moments that taste sweetest on a palate jaded by caviar and big killings on the market.

'Domestic escalators' is not, I ought perhaps to warn gentlemen of fortune, a well-chosen phrase for echo work. It came into my mind at random, and is a shade too iambic for good results. Quick dactyls, Gilbert White observes after experiment with a Selborne echo (public, as I read it), succeed best, such a line as *'Tityre, tu patulae recubans. . . .'* giving a far more satisfactory answer than the 'slow, heavy, embarrassed spondees' of *'Monstrum horrendum, informe, ingens. . . .'* Millionaires whose Virgil is rusty may not care to arouse the loquacious nymph with hexameters, but the general principle is one they may like to keep in mind. A shout of 'Sears, Roebuck is down one-sixteenth!' for instance, could well disappoint the listening tycoon, whereas some such lilting phrase as 'Bethlehem Steel and Kennecott Copper are rocketing up to the skies', though inaccurate, should come back prettily enough.

Anyone who has ever opened the *Natural History* will agree that it is difficult, once launched, to avoid turning the pages to see what happens next. Not that there is any 'story' – far from it. The book consists of a series of letters written to two friends, and part of its charm lies in its extraordinary diversity. The author had a catholic curiosity. The statement that worms are 'much addicted to venery,' in Letter XXXV, leads one insensibly on to leprosy and oysters in Letter XXXVII. So I take no personal credit for discovering, some fifteen pages after the Reverend White's timely hint about echoes (Letter XXXVIII), the following stimulant in Letter XLIV:

> Gentlemen who have outlets might contrive to make ornament subservient to utility; a pleasing eye-trap might also contribute to promote science: an obelisk in a garden or park might be both an embellishment and an heliotrope.
>
> Any person that is curious, and enjoys the advantage of a good horizon, might, with little trouble, make two heliotropes; the one for the winter, the other for the summer solstice: and these two erections might be constructed with very little expense; for two pieces of timber frame-work, about ten or twelve feet high, and four feet broad at the base, and close lined with plank, would answer the purpose.

I suppose you might search Texas from end to end and fail to find a millionaire with both a summer and a winter heliotrope on his estate; in all the world I doubt whether there is a single man who possesses these two embellishments *and* a custom-built echo. Texans, for all I know, may think that a heliotrope is merely a flower and not, as it seems to have been in Gilbert White's day, a construction for promoting science by observing the south-westerly and north-westerly limits of the setting sun. Here, then, is scope for means and imagination, for individuality without ostentation. For observe that the visible apparatus, as White is at pains to state, is by no means expensive. A dog kennel here, a timber framework there, and the thing is done. It is the setting that puts these luxuries beyond the reach of the ordinary man. For your echo you must have two hills of a gentle declivity some few hundred yards apart, with your kennels and barns suitably disposed about them to promote reverberation, and a canal or lake between. But your heliotropes demand a good natural horizon, since no man can observe the extreme westering of the sun if some hillock intervenes. Thus your declivities, as I deduce, must face north and south, leaving a level plain to westward for the heliotropes. A further complication arises in the siting of the mansion itself to command the winter heliotrope. 'The erection for the former,' Gilbert White well says (referring to the heliotrope, rather than the mansion), 'should, if possible, be placed within sight of some window in the common sitting parlour; because men, at that dead season of the year, are usually within doors at the close of the day.' This is certainly a valid point, if the winter heliotrope is to be relished to the full.

Of the summer heliotrope our authority merely says that it '. . . might be fixed for any given spot in the garden or outlet: whence the owner might contemplate, in a fine summer's evening, the utmost extent that the sun makes to the northward at the season of the longest days. Now nothing would be necessary but to place these two objects with so much exactness, that the westerly limb of the sun, at setting, might but just clear the winter heliotrope to the west of it on the shortest day; and that the whole disc of the sun, at the longest day, might exactly at setting also clear the summer heliotrope to the north of it.' Something else, in fact, *will* be necessary, as millionaires who have followed me attentively will already have realised, if we are to achieve the highest degree of delight from our combination of heliotropes with echo – a synthesis, by the way, that Gilbert White, for all his imaginative genius, does not seem to have envisaged. We shall certainly require that the summer heliotrope be sited at the *centrum phonicum*. Only thus will our Midsummer Day guests have the felicity of hearing their exclamations of astonishment at the apparition of the solstice echoed and reechoed on the soft evening air before they make their uphill way – by escalator? by an *outdoor carpeted* escalator? – back to the common sitting parlour.

This, I think it will be agreed, is no ordinary outlet, no gimcrack contrivance unworthy of a man of substance. A lake faultily sited, a single dog kennel out of line, and all falls to the ground. A man might keep his mind healthily occupied for years, and run, I daresay, through twenty or thirty millions before he had the thing working to perfection. And what deep-seated satisfaction when it was done! What are a dozen swimming pools or a hundred domestic escalators against a set-up like this?

Virgil claims that echoes are injurious to bees. Gilbert White denies it, arguing that bees are in no way capable of being affected by sounds. 'I have often,' he writes in Letter XXXVII, 'tried my own with a large speaking-trumpet held close to their hives, and with such an exertion of voice as would have hailed a ship at the distance of a mile, and still these insects pursued their various employments undisturbed, and without showing the least sensibility or resentment.' The word 'often' so casually slipped in here well displays the true naturalist's tenacity of purpose and disregard of what the neighbours may be thinking, but as a test of the toxicity of echoes the procedure falls short of conviction. I suggest, without wishing to over-refine on the pleasures available to the rich, that owners of private echoes might gain an added diversion from noting their effect on the bee – particularly perhaps during the *longueurs* of the off-seasons when no solstice presents itself for observation. The hives should be set at or near the *centrum phonicum* and should be observed from afar, perhaps from some window in the sitting parlour, in case the bees should be found to show sensibility. A guest or expendable gardener would no doubt be willing to set the echoes flying; nor need the experimenter's distance from the insects preclude accuracy of observation. Any gentleman of fortune could, with little trouble or expense, provide himself with an apiscope.

Robin in a Cage

Anybody not interested in robins can skip all this.

I was working in a cage, pricking up the earth round two or three dozen strawberry plants we encourage under the protection of a post-and-chicken-wire structure, when the robin came and perched on one of the cross-struts above my head. He sang to me, the sad little winter song of his kind.

I am familiar with this bird. Part of my small garden lies within his territory, and he attends me closely whenever I stir the soil, knowing with the inherited lore of a thousand generations that a man with a fork equals worms. I am also fairly familiar with birds in general, having studied them through binoculars and read about them in a surprising number of books. I know that the obvious explanation for almost everything they do is wrong. I have read endlessly, endlessly about bird-behaviour, about inherited and acquired characteristics, about responses to stimuli and ritual grass-pulling and the significance of the red spot on a herring gull's bill. I have read Tinbergen, you see; also *Animals as Social Beings* by Adolf Portmann and *Bird* by Lois and Louis Darling and all twelve volumes of Bannerman's *Birds of the British Isles* and a monograph on the sparrow and David Lack's book on the robin itself, and I am well aware that to write, as I have, that a bird sang 'to me' is an obnoxious example of anthropomorphism or, if you prefer it, the pathetic fallacy. He sang to defend his territory, or to practise, or in anger. It was a hormone, not I, that triggered him off.

The robin wanted to get in. The stimulus provided by a man with a fork excited his digestive juices, never long dormant, and caused him to hop about on the wire above my head in a frustrated kind of way. After a bit he tried the sides of the cage, prancing and fluttering about at ground level or making an occasional useless sortie higher up. He also investigated the far end pretty minutely, hauling off for brief spells to revive himself with song or some other displacement activity and then hurtling back to his task with a desperation that increased with his appetite. These manoeuvres made it hard for me to concentrate on my work.

'Try the door, old chap,' I said. 'It's open.'

The vibrations of a bird's tympanum are transmitted across the middle ear by the columella, whence they pass into the fluid of the perilymphatic duct and so, by means of the sensory cells of the basilar papilla, to the auditory nerve. Many song-birds can hear sounds from as high a frequency as 20,000 cycles per second down to 50 cycles. These facts, however, are without significance in the present context, since the number of sounds that convey any precise meaning to a bird (if I may use so unscientific a term as 'meaning' to suggest the power to call out some functional response) is strictly limited, and does not include the phrase 'Try the door, old chap.' The robin was therefore behaving with textbook correctness in continuing to try the back and sides.

I wish I could say the same for my own behaviour, which now became as confused and irrational as that of a man who has never opened an ornithological book in his life. 'Not up there, damn it,' I shouted. 'Come round this way, you fool!' And I made a sweeping gesture with the fork in the direction of the cage door. 'In *here*, man.'

Sweeping gestures nearly always stimulate alarm responses in birds, leading to flight, which may be followed by preening, bill cleaning, low-intensity regurgitation and even displacement nest-building. They never get robins through cage doors. Seeing the bird fly off to a nearby wheelbarrow and begin to sing in what I thought was rather a ritualistic way, I took a grip of myself. What would Niko Tinbergen think of me, I asked myself, or Adolf Portmann, or David Lack, or Eric Ennion, or Peter Scott or any of the great ones: trying to communicate with a bird by shouting at it and waving a fork! These shaming thoughts acted upon me as what we call a 'releaser' and flooded my face and throat with so bright a red that I half expected the robin to adopt a threat posture. But it had gone off to stir up some leaves under a hedge, and I decided to get on with my digging.

Never in my life have I turned up so many worms. Often, when the robin is close beside me, out in the open, I deliberately search for worms for him and find nothing. Now I could not put the fork into the ground without heaving up a whole family, many of them fat and welted, all skittish and wriggling. Platoons of worms. The sight of so much waste sickened me, and I looked away – to discover that the robin was back, clinging to the outside of the wire with bulging eyes and salivary glands (which secrete no digestive enzymes) that must have been stimulated to an overpowering degree. There was an air of frozen desperation about the creature. 'A thousand million damns,' I said, and strode outside the cage.

'Look!' I said to the robin. 'Here I am outside. With you. *Out!* Now watch.' I went back into the cage. 'And here I am, inside again. see? *In!*' It was like speaking to a foreigner. I spoke slowly, accentuating the important words. I went out and in again, repeating the procedure, while the robin watched me with his head on one side. I do not know what madness led me, who am so wise in the ways of birds, to do this thing: to expect the bird, whose learning ability is notoriously feeble, to carry out the immensely complicated processes of observation, memory-retention, self-identification and translation into action that I was requiring of it. All I know is that after my sixth exit and entry the robin flew off to the far end of the cage and sought frantically there for admittance, while I went up to the house for a pipe.

When I got back he was inside, waiting for me. 'So there you are,' I said, glad of his company, though not so besotted as to imagine that he was glad of mine, or indeed capable of anything that we should call emotion. I then noticed a curious thing. Although perfectly unafraid when within two feet of me in the open this bird could not stand my proximity within wire. A robin redbreast in a cage, I have to tell Blake, is all right until a man joins him. He then becomes extremely uneasy, or rather – since we ought to avoid language that suggests the possession of *feelings* – he is stimulated into a series of rapid flights towards the roof, back and sides of the enclosure. Not towards the door. He has a horror of doors. Unable for long to stand this agitated fluttering and commotion I threw down my fork and left the cage for the last time. 'Have it your own way,' I said. 'It's all yours now.'

At once he came out and, sitting on the wheelbarrow's rim, began to sing his sad little winter song. A sentimentalist would have called it his farewell; but I am not a sentimentalist. I am an ornithologist, sort of, and all I wanted was a good, reviving displacement activity, with very little ritual water in it.

Dusty Answer

1980

It all depends on whether you prefer sluggish and more or less evolutionary causes for great events or one great crash that does the job in the twinkling of an eye. Myself, I am on the side of the Big Bang. And not just to explain the creation of the universe, important though that was in its way.

Take Knossos. Many theories have been advanced for the destruction of the Palace of Minos sometime in the fifteenth century BC. Some say it was the Mycenaeans, others blame it on a Cretan revolution. Professors argue for and against the simultaneous collapse of such well-sited subsidiary structures as Phaestos, Mallia, and Hagia Triada, disagreeing violently about the actual date of all this havoc and indulging in much heated talk about stratification. But there is no need for us to get bogged down in a quagmire of clay tablets, Late Minoan II vases, labyrinthine legends, and the rest, when the whole problem can be solved by one vast bang on the island of Santorini, about seventy-five miles north of Knossos.

Pretty well the whole of Santorini (or Thera, as the Greeks preferred to call it) blew up in 1470 BC, or thereabouts, in a spectacular volcanic eruption, and one theory is that the resulting tidal wave devastated the Minoan settlements on the facing coast of Crete. 'A glance at the map,' says Mr J. V. Luce, in his *The End of Atlantis*, 'will show how exposed the whole northern coast of Crete is to waves coming from Thera.' So down went Mallia, Amnisos, Katsamba, and a whole string of less distinguished seaside resorts. Knossos itself, lying farther inland and better protected, 'would have had a chance,' continues Mr Luce, going a bit chicken in my opinion, 'to escape annihilation,' but he admits that 'very large waves could have washed around it.' And what about Phaestos and Hagia Triada, snugly on the south coast or near it, as another glance at the map will show, but also due for destruction at this time? Courage! We must not forget that a top-rate volcano can do more than stir up the adjacent waters. 'Other possibilities are: earthquakes, preceding or following the eruption; blast damage to upper stories combined with the breaking down of roofs and upper floors by a heavy fallout of ash; pillaging by the starving survivors of the disaster.' Well done, Luce! There is nothing like a thick layer of ash for wiping out a civilization, especially if, 'as seems probable, the eruption took place in the period June-August,' when 'all vegetation in central and eastern Crete would have suffered severe damage' and 'crops still in the fields are likely to have been completely destroyed.' Add the defoliation of 'olives and vines,' and there you are. As whole-hearted and all-embracing an explanation of a difficult crux in the Bronze Age as you could wish to find. I reckon this to have been the most labour-saving Big Bang in the known history of the world since the original one, in ten billion BC, or whenever.

Or, rather, I did so reckon. But now, to usher in the nineteen-eighties, comes splendid news about an asteroid that killed off all the sizable dinosaurs some sixty-five million years ago. The demise of these ponderous reptiles has vexed generations of zoologists, palaeontologists, and palaeoecologists. Something out of the way was felt to be needed to account for the extinction of creatures up to eighty feet or more in length and weighing around forty tons when fully fit. You can't put it down to an outbreak of malaria, such as (some used to say) brought about the decline and fall of the Roman Empire. After all, these dinosaurs had been around, lording it over the earth, for upward of a hundred and forty million years and must have got the hang of coping, for all their small heads and elongated nervous systems, with minor disorders. There were no Mycenaeans about, either, to blame for the disaster. So some palaeontologists have been arguing that it must have been the up-and-coming mammals that outsmarted the dinosaurs, though others say rats to that, because there is no evidence of any contemporary mammal in those quaint Mesozoic times larger than 'a shrew-like creature only a few centimetres long.' 'It is just possible,' observes David Attenborough, in *Life on Earth*, 'that such a small creature could have preyed on dinosaur eggs,' but he can't credit it with a totally genocidal appetite.

So it must have been the cold weather. After a hundred and forty million years of gracious living, one of those well-known bleak periods set in, and down went the dinosaurs with hypothermia – many of them to fall into the Paluxy Creek, in Texas, *en route* to the Dinosaur National Monument museum. Others huddled together up in Montana to await the end. H.G. Wells, as long ago as 1922, when warmer days had returned, wrote, 'How safe and eternal the sunshine and abundance must have seemed, how assured the wallowing prosperity of the dinosaurs and the flapping abundance of the flying lizards! And then the mysterious rhythms and accumulating forces of the universe began to turn against that quasi-eternal stability. That run of luck for life was running out.' Yes indeed. And Attenborough, a little more prosaically, agrees with him, pointing out that '. . . a succession of bitterly cold nights could have drained a big dinosaur of its heat beyond all recovery. With its body badly chilled, it might not be able to summon sufficient energy to move its huge bulk and browse.' *Exeunt* the herbivores, and with them, of course, the carnivores that relied on them for sustenance.

It is a pitiful picture this – of shivering diplodoci and famished tyrannosauri dragging their slow lengths along through the lush, though rime-encrusted, vegetation, too feeble even to munch – nor is it one that I care to contemplate or feel prepared to accept. What was evolution supposed to be thinking of? This cold snap can hardly have come overnight, and would surely have advanced gradually enough for the wiser dinosaurs to flee before it or to evolve some sort of protective covering, as did the woolly rhinoceros during a more recent spell of inclement weather. No, what is called for here is a cataclysm of more than Minoan proportions, and we must all feel grateful to the Lawrence Berkeley Laboratory of California for providing one.

My information on this second Big Bang comes from a report in an English newspaper of the proceedings last January of the American Association for the Advancement of Science, and is not as fully documented as I could wish. My understanding is that an asteroid, probably from one of the Apollo groups of planetoids, crashed into Earth at the end of the Cretaceous period, terminating the Age of Reptiles and the Mesozoic Era in one tremendous swipe. This asteroid – 'weighing some 13 trillion tons,' says my paper airily, 'roughly equal to the weight of the Greater London Area to a depth of 10 miles' (fancy knowing the weight of *that*!) – would have struck the earth at several thousand miles per hour and '. . . would have thrown a hundred times its own weight of dust up into the atmosphere.'

That is a great deal of dust. In fact, I can tell you straightaway that it is 'more than 1,600 times what was released by the volcanic explosion of the island of Krakatoa in 1883' and '. . . would have blackened the sky, turning days into nights, for three to five years.'

Good old Krakatoa. As cataclysms go, that famous upheaval came too late to solve any vexed historical or palaeo-problems; one looks in vain for the hitherto unexplained collapse of a palace or two around 1883, or the total extinction of the Flying Dragon of Java. The more modest role of Krakatoa is to show what can be done in the way of stirring up dust and tidal waves – to act as a kind of 'control,' as scientists say, for the better estimation of the effects of less well documented cataclysms. Mr Luce says that '. . . the evidence of the great eruption of Krakatoa in AD 1883 is crucial for any attempt to reconstruct what happened on Thera in the Late Bronze Age ,' and he makes '. . . no apology for going into the Krakatoa eruption in considerable detail,' I make no apology, either, for *not* going into it in considerable detail, merely wishing to note that the resulting tidal wave was vast and that the fallout of ash and pumice plunged Batavia, a hundred and sixty-five kilometres away, into complete darkness. Small wonder, then, if Knossos, at a mere hundred and twenty kilometres from the equivalent disturbance on Thera, was never quite the same again. And, more to the point, multiply Batavia's discomfort by a factor of sixteen hundred, as instructed by the scientists of the Lawrence Berkeley Laboratory, and one can see that the dinosaurs were out of luck.

All the same, I am a bit puzzled by the thirteen hundred trillion tons of dust said to have been thrown up by the Apollo asteroid. It's not the calculation that worries me – any competent scientist can weigh dust – but where the dust came from. That a volcano like Krakatoa or Thera can produce a vast quantity of powdered debris from its subterranean resources one readily accepts. But an asteroid is not a volcano, however many times one multiplies one by the other. Where did it land? In some Cretaceous dust bowl? My paper is silent on the point. And, anyway, my picture of Mesozoic earth – one I shall not easily relinquish – is wet rather than dry. Besides a full complement of oceans, so essential from the earliest times for the production of life, I see great forests of tree ferns and cycads, all hot and steaming in a damp, tropical way: typical dinosaur country, interspersed with brackish lagoons in which ichthyosaurs and plesiosaurs splash and dive. Wallowing, to borrow a word from H.G. Wells, is rife. Very well, then. Hit this lot with an asteroid where you will, even in the June-August period, and whence comes the dust? If it fell in the seas, as seems most likely, I'd expect a tidal wave high enough to overtop the tallest tyrannosaurus that ever browsed and powerful enough to go round and round the earth a dozen times; if it fell among the swampy vegetation, we have to envisage such a splattering of mud mixed with fragmented cycads, mosses, shrew-like creatures, old megalosaurus bones, and other detritus as was never seen since the world began. This asteroid, moreover, at the speed it was going must have been pretty hot on impact (though my newspaper makes no mention of it), so that I reckon the mixture thrown up must have been at least two hundred times as unpleasant as anything that rained down on Batavia – or on Knossos, for that matter.

Such then, in brief, is what I hope will come to be known as the Anti-Dust Postulate. Blinded by boiling mud, their nostrils choked with flying moss, the enormous herds of stegosauri, triceratopses, and the rest lacked the will and the means to escape the ensuing tidal wave, which hurtled them many times around the globe – 'rolled round,' as Wordsworth has it in another context, 'with rocks, and stones, and trees' – and finally cast them up, in a hideous tangle of scaly tails, bony frills, huge horns, and backbones as long as cricket pitches, at suitable sites in Texas and Montana. Who shall blame them if, after that, they simply gave up and allowed themselves to be covered by Tertiary deposits for another sixty-five million years.?

It may seem a little headstrong for a layman to take issue, on the basis of a short news report, with the conclusions of the Lawrence Berkeley Laboratory, but I just can't swallow all that dust. From three to five years, they say, it hung about, depriving the plants of solar radiation and so starving the dinosaurs of their foodstuffs, while permitting 'smaller animals, weighing under about 25 lbs, including the squirrel-sized ancestors of Man' to survive 'by living on rotting vegetation.' It isn't good enough. No ancestor of mine ever lived for three years on rotting vegetation. I can accept a dusty answer for the troubles of Knossos, but what is sauce for the minotaur is not necessarily sauce for the dinosaur. These professors, it seems to me, have simply chucked away the inherent advantages of a first-rate cataclysm and turned what could have been a worthily sensational end to a hundred and forty million years of world supremacy into a sunless death in a huge heap of highly odoriferous silage. Over-anxious to explain how all those large saurians could be demolished without a simultaneous extinction of the emergent mammals, my sources make bold to state that 'plant seeds would have regerminated after the return of the sunlight . . . and surviving animal species [would have] soon repopulated the land and sea.' 'This,' one of the professors is reported to have said, 'fits what is observed in the fossil record.'

My own mud-and-flood theory preserves our ancestors without recourse to any such dusty generalisations. Obviously, a few nimble squirrel-sized creatures (or shrew-like, if you prefer to follow Attenborough) scrambled up a handy mountain and, shaking off any stray particles of mud and moss, sat there on the top above the tidal-wave level and settled down to await the return of more normal evolutionary times. They probably ate nuts, which would be washed up in quantity as the floods receded. This fits what is observed in the Biblical record. Near enough.

Layman Falls into Black Hole

1981. This is a hideously complicated inquiry – hitherto unpublished, and no wonder – into the origins of the Universe. I include it on the off chance that some astrophysical reader will explain to me where my reasoning, such as it is, goes most disastrously astray.

Dr Spinrad, of the University of California, astronomer, has got to come to my assistance – assuming, that is, that he is a kindly man who would not wish to be responsible for permanently unhinging the mind of a fairly inoffensive fellow human being.

I say *fairly* inoffensive because quite recently, hardly a millisecond or so ago as astrophysicists reckon time, I felt obliged to throw cold water on a cloud of dust raised by the Lawrence Berkeley Laboratory of California, and I have an uneasy fear (minimal as is my knowledge of the set-up over there) that Dr Spinrad may have close links with the Laboratory. I mean he might have shared any resentment caused by my refusal to believe that all the dinosaurs were wiped out sixty-five million years ago by the detritus thrown up by an asteroid. Rightly, too. I was myself conscious at the time, as one whose knowledge of physics was limited to some desultory reading of Aristotle at Oxford and a faint recollection of rolling steel balls down an inclined plane while at school, of a certain temerity, impertinence even, in challenging the conclusions of a phalanx of far-off Professors and PhDs. So let me say at once that I do not for one moment intend to aggravate the offence, to add insult to injury or to pile Pelion on Ossa, by querying one jot or tittle of the recent discoveries announced (in the *Astrophysical Journal* and elsewhere) by Dr Spinrad – even though his announcements have left me in a state of bleak intergalactic despair. I just need help.

What then has Dr Spinrad been up to? He has discovered, with the aid of his associates at Berkeley, three huge previously unknown galaxies whose light has taken no less than 10,000 million years to reach us, which is a matter of 2,000 million years longer than any light hitherto noted from such sources. It would take about a million million stars, Dr Spinrad says, to produce the brightness observed in each of these galaxies, compared with the mere 100,000 million in our own little Milky Way affair, but even so the University observatory needed a 'special scanner' that 'captures and stores minute quantities of light' to detect the existence of these monstrosities. So far, so far. Nothing to worry me in all this, and I should like to send to the doctor and his associates, across eight thousand miles of sea and land – which is no more than 0.0000000013 of a light year, rightly regarded – my warm congratulations on a pretty smart bit of observation.

But that, unfortunately, is not the end of the matter. Scientists, not content with making observations, like to draw conclusions and propound theories; and here, as reported from Berkeley and kindly passed on to me in simplified form by the London *Times*, are some of them.

'The discovery, they said' – this is *The Times* saying what 'Astronomers at the University of California' said – 'supports the Big Bang theory of how the universe began, which has been challenged by some scientists in recent years.

'"Evidence from these farthest galaxies," a university spokesman said' – and now we've got *The Times* saying what the spokesman actually said, in *oratio recta*, hence these tiresome double quotes – '"strongly supports a theory suggesting that a primordial explosion or Big Bang occurred about 18 billion years ago and was followed by the formation of stars and galaxies within about two billion years."

'The light observed and measured by the scientists has been travelling through space at the speed of six million million miles per year for about 10,000 million years. Since astronomers believe the universe is 18,000 million years old, the discovery means astronomers "are looking more than halfway back in time toward the moment many of them believe marks the beginning of the universe", the report said.'

(There seem to be rather a lot of people talking, don't you think? We've heard what 'Astronomers at the University' said and what 'a university spokesman' said, and now we've got 'the report' chipping in with its contribution. Nor is this all. The best, as we shall see, is yet to be.)

'Dr Spinrad said' – Aha! The fountainhead at last – 'Dr Spinrad said improved equipment is becoming available to see objects another 2000 or 3000 light years away. Not too far in the future, they might be able to measure light from galaxies 16,000 light years away. Such light would have been created when the universe was only 2000 million years old and thus might unravel once and for all the puzzle of how it all began.'

Very well, then, what am I making all this fuss about? Dr Spinrad's arithmetic, in the last quoted paragraph, is surely within the grasp even of an Aristotelian. Obviously, if light from some object takes billions of years to reach us, we are getting information about the nature of that object when it was billions of years younger. Astronomers, you might say, are in the same position as the recipient of the photograph of an old friend's son, aged two, that has been delayed fifty years or so in the post. Both parties, if I may employ so bold a phrase, are getting near a glimpse of the embryo stage; indeed, the former – though not, one hopes, the latter – might one day reach it. Listen to this:

'Eventually, scientists might get to the very edge of the universe and then determine whether we are in an "open" world that is expanding indefinitely or a "closed" universe, fated to collapse on itself eventually, the report said.'

By 'the very edge of the universe' I take the report (or the astronomers, or the spokesman, or most likely Dr Spinrad himself) to mean galaxies that are the full eighteen billion light years away and are transmitting information about themselves dating back to Year One of the universe. This completes my mental disorientation and prompts me, none too soon, to express my dismay in the form of a series of propositions, some of which *must* be false. The question that Dr Spinrad has to answer is, which?

1. The universe started with a Big Bang eighteen billion years ago, which, after the nature of explosions threw out a lot of material of some kind, probably gaseous (or, if the Lawrence Berkeley Laboratory had anything to do with it, dust).

2. This material coagulated in a couple of billion years into stars and galaxies which set off in all directions at ever increasing velocities.

3. Nobody tells me where the Big Bang took place, but I cannot be far wrong in supposing that it occurred at a sizable spot marked X.

4. It would be absurdly reactionary, geocentric and neo-Ptolemaic to believe that X was *here*, i.e. in our own galaxy, and even if it was we shouldn't be there now.

5. It would be more reasonable to put X somewhere about midway between us (E) and one of these titanic Spinrad galaxies (SG), but *in that case* and assuming (and why shouldn't I?) that both parties have been receding

from X with equal velocities, half the ten billion years we have had to wait for the light from SG has been due to our own recession. That light took only five billion years to get back to X where it all began, which looks pretty odd to me because what has its source been up to during the missing thirteen billion years? In any case, SG must be either younger or older than we were led to expect, depending on the degree of incomprehension reached at any given moment by the spokesman at my desk, and consequently more, or on the other hand less, useless to Dr Spinrad in his search for the origins of the universe.

6. Proposition No. 5 is so clearly the work of an unbalanced mind that it will be better to go right out to the very edge of the universe and see what happens there. That 'equal velocities' assumption must have been wrong, otherwise all the galaxies would be equidistant from each other, or anyway from X, which would either make a nonsense of the claim to have discovered more and more distant galaxies *or*, perhaps, make it possible to fix the position of X, and I am in no state to contemplate either contingency. I therefore propose to anticipate the day when Dr Spinrad has got his scanner really ticking over and is able to pick up the light from some object 18 billion light years away, give or take a few millions. He will then be looking at the very beginning of all things, at the primordial stuff of which the universe was composed; indeed, if he isn't careful, he may be looking at the Big Bang itself, and I should advise him to wear dark glasses. It ought to be quite a spectacle.

7. All will then be revealed, and all our difficulties will disappear in, as one might say, one blinding flash of very minute quantities of light. Or will they? Not mine. Not by a long – an astronomically long – chalk. I just don't understand how this primordial object got so far away, or rather how its light has been so long arriving.

Because when it was primordial, so were we, and at that time, shortly after the Big Bang, all the elements of the universe were by definition close together, or anyway closer than they were ever to be again once we all started expanding this way and that. So why the devil didn't this inchoate light reach us billions of years ago and push on elsewhere into space? I feel myself on the verge of stating a Law as inverse as anything perpetrated by Kepler or Newton, viz. that *the nearer two objects are to each other, the longer light takes to pass between them.* Dr Spinrad will by now, if he is still with me, be beginning to realise what he has done.

8. Proposition 7 has left me in such a tizzy that I am inclined to clutch at some very far-flung straws. If Dr Spinrad's scanner, working to the limits of its powers, detects the Big Bang, or anyway its immediate consequences, at the 'very edge of the universe', does it not follow that we have pretty well pinned down the position of X? But if so, what on earth was the Big Bang thinking of to happen right out there? A good half of its precious material would be hurled clean out of the universe at the first puff, and be lost for ever. This does not seem right to me. It's wasteful. And another thing – suppose Dr Spinrad turns his scanner through 180 degrees of azimuth (which I am sure is well within his capabilities) and picks up another agglomeration of pristine matter at the opposite extreme of the universe, where are we then? We are in danger of postulating *two* Big Bangs, thirty-six billion light years apart, which is more than I can stomach. Indeed, if the Doctor continues to rotate on his own axis, scanning the while, he may very well hit upon a whole series, hundreds, perhaps an infinity of potential Big Bangs, some of them perhaps even bigger than others.

9. We are fast approaching the extreme edge of insanity, further than which my personal scanner cannot probe. I therefore withdraw this madcap notion of an

infinity of Bangs and substitute one continuous, simultaneous, gigantic explosion circular rather than globular, running right round the rim of the universe – a vast circumference of fire, such as was envisaged, with rare foresight, by Lucretius, in his famous phrase about the 'flammantia moenia mundi'. Like it or not, this is a magnificent conception, not unworthy to produce a universe of galaxies and stars and planets, with *homo sapiens* (and in particular the astronomers at Berkeley) as its ultimate triumph.

10. It won't do, though, because it cuts clean across the 'expanding universe' theory, and I don't believe Dr Spinrad would like that. Anybody who has heard of the 'red shift' knows that all the galaxies so far discovered are *receding*, and the further the faster, from which even I can deduce that a universe which began at its own extremities and expanded outwards would be a total failure. A bang, and then not even a whimper. So I am impaled on the horns of a hideous dilemma. *Either* the expanding universe began at its own edges, where Dr Spinrad apparently expects to find evidence of its origins – in which case it doesn't exist, *or* it began somewhere inside, in which case its first-born light had no business to take so long to reach us.

11. *Or* – since this turns out to be a three-horned dilemma – it is not in fact an expanding but a *contracting* universe, which started round the rim and has been whizzing inwards ever since. The difficulty here, of course, is that a whole bevy of astronomers have to be accused of getting their calculations wrong, of mistaking a centripetal rush of galaxies for a centrifugal one. Is it conceivable that they have all got their red shifts on inside out?

12. No, it isn't. So would you please, Dr Spinrad, be so kind as to hold out a helping hand – and soon. There is not, at the rate at which my mind is now receding from its hinges, much time.

A Walk in Massachusetts

For the state of near panic I got into last spring, in a wood about five miles from Groton, Massachusetts, I am indebted, in the main, to John Hersey, Clifford H. Pope, and a lady in a small sports car. The lady took me to the wood. 'If you are interested in birds,' she told me, 'it's the ideal place. A kind of nature preserve. Nobody ever goes there, so you'll be quite undisturbed, and herons nest on the island.' She had found me beside the road, in a pleasant, swampy area just across the Ayer-Hollis branch freight railroad line, had offered me a ride, and had quickly discovered that I was British and a bird-watcher.

'It is extremely kind of you to bother,' I said. It is always extremely kind of Americans to bother, and no counter has yet been devised by visiting Englishmen to stop them from doing it.

We drove for a couple of miles along tarmac roads, branched off on a dirt road between farmsteads, and jogged and jolted down a rutted sand track into a forest of conifers. A pair of what I thought might be red-shouldered hawks wheeled in the flawless June sky. The track ended at a stretch of sluggish backwater, and there I got out. I had only to follow the river to the left, the lady told me, and I would find that it curled round on itself and would, in time, lead me back to the main road. 'Look out for poison ivy!' she called as she turned the car. 'There's a lot of it in these woods.'

'Right,' I said. 'Thanks. Oh, by the way – I say –

How does one—'

'It kind of grows in threes,' she cried, waved, and was gone.

It was intensely hot. No breath of air penetrated the close-set trees. Nothing moved, and no birds sang. An island across the water appeared to be heron-less. There was, however, a discernible path running by the water's edge, and I was glad to follow it. Poison ivy does not grow in Britain, nor did I recollect much about it save that it is not recognisable as ivy and that its lightest touch leads to intense irritation, bloating of the body, and possible collapse. But a man who walks with circumspection along a path, keeping in the middle of it and on no account sitting down to rest, has little to fear. I pressed forward, holding the arms close to the body and noting, without excitement, some curious round bumps on a derelict tree trunk half submerged in the water. My mind was occupied at this time with the need for tobacco and with the obvious folly of lighting a cigarette in this crackling tinderbox of a forest.

The bumps slid off and poised themselves an inch or so below the surface, extruding stringy necks and bluntish yellow heads. I watched them with mounting interest. America is full of differences for an Englishman. New York is instantly distinguishable from London. Lobster tastes better. The Budd Highliner, on its run from Boston to Ayer, makes a wailing noise at crossings that would never be tolerated in England. But these differences are neither unexpected nor radical. Turtles are something else altogether. Turtles are downright un-English. Free, wild, and treading water gently by an old tree trunk, they affect the mind far more powerfully than a Pullman-car attendant or even a copy of the *Herald Tribune*. For the first time, looking at them, I became aware that I was on a vast continent – exotic, tropical, rich in the possibility of surprises undreamed of in Shropshire or Kent.

I was not in any way frightened. The British, for all their loss of prestige, are not yet afraid of small turtles. The note that I immediately made, on the flyleaf of my pocket *Field Guide to the Birds (Eastern)*, is in front of me now, and the writing is, for a man menaced by poison ivy and with sweat trickling off his nose, admirably firm. 'Yellow on head,' it reads. 'Red on neck and at sides of shell. Fond of sunning. Submerges when startled.' It is the first field note I ever made on turtles, and for identification purposes is insufficiently detailed. But at the time I thought it would do. Back at home, I had recently acquired a book by Clifford H. Pope, with descriptions and photographs of innumerable species of turtles; somewhere there, I thought, these yellow-headed turtles would be.

My mind associates very readily when I am alone in great heat in foreign woods. It would have been difficult, whatever the circumstances, to recall Clifford H. Pope's turtles without reflecting that the same fine volume, *The Reptile World*, contains about a hundred photographs of snakes. Pretty nearly all of them flashed on my mental retina simultaneously. Not all, of course, infest America. Cobras I could shrug off, and also, I rather hoped, the dreaded Russell's viper. But there were plenty left. With particular vividness, there recurred to me a picture of a long, thin snake looped and coiled about a branch, and some excellent high-speed photographs of a rattlesnake striking a balloon. Just such a target would be provided, coincidentally, by a man under the influence of poison ivy. . . .

Preoccupied with these thoughts, I failed to notice that the conifers had receded and the path had petered out. All about me were deciduous trees whose branches trailed curious, often trifoliate, parasitical growths. Between their trunks grew low bushes and taller shrubs, mostly in kind of threes, while underfoot the ground lay deep in the debris, the leaf mould and withered branches, of centuries of decay, so that it was hard to tell where best to tread. Some sort of willows, their gnarled roots suggestive of alligators, drooped over the stagnant waters.

I am glad to think that I retained, at this stage, a sense of proportion. It could be that of all the countless varieties of venomous snakes indigenous to America so sinuously described by Mr Pope, no more than three or four were ever found in Massachusetts. *A Field Guide to the Snakes (Eastern)* might be an altogether slimmer volume than my bird book. As for the poison ivy, a touch of cutaneous eruption would be a small price to pay for a glimpse of the island where herons once nested. Still, I thought it best to turn the cuffs of my trousers down over my ankles, in case the ivy was a ground creeper. I kept my hands in my pockets against the risk of waist-high bushes. For the exposed face and neck, nothing could be done except to keep a constant watch for trailing growths when passing under trees; I should be looking up in any case, because no naturalist wants to miss his first sight of a long, thin snake looped and coiled about a branch. The difficulty here was that the urge to look down was no less strong. 'Watch where you step' was the phrase that came back to me from Clifford H. Pope's useful section on snake-bite prevention and treatment.

I suppose that any resident of Groton who had seen me mincing along thus protected, looking down and up before every step and shrinking away with loathing from every vegetable contact, would have laughed uproariously. The lady with the sports car would have been in stitches. Local knowledge makes a world of difference. Here in England, where a mild rash from the stinging nettle is the gravest probable consequence of a country walk, I stride along as briskly as any Grotonian. I should have done the same, I daresay, in Massachusetts had I read Mr Pope's book more carefully (or not at all), or had the lady in the sports car not been kind enough to bother.

Oddly, it was neither of these two that finally broke my nerve. It happened that in swerving away from a particularly vicious three-pronged attack from overhead I put my foot on some round, slippery object (perhaps a dead branch) and, so rapidly was my mind associating by this time, I actually recalled a whole passage from John Hersey's novel *The Marmot Drive* while still in the act of falling backward into a prehensile bush of a type not found on my side of the Atlantic. By pure chance, not having the gift of divination, I had borrowed this book from the ship's library on my way over to the United States. It is recommended reading for anyone not contemplating a walk in Massachusetts. For me, it would have been better had the scene of the great round-up of groundhogs been set in some other state; better still if the heroine had not fallen into a thicket during the drive.

She was not, of course, actually eaten alive by groundhogs. She was not even afraid of being eaten alive, because she knew that some of her friends in the long line of beaters ahead would soon notice her absence and come thrashing back. She was a calm, sensible sort of girl, and soon realised that the more she struggled the more deeply she would enmesh herself in the spiny thicket. So she just lay still and waited. I was unable to emulate her confident self-possession. One of the delights of a nature preserve, as the sports-car lady had pointed out, is that nobody ever goes there.

It would be wrong to give the impression that I remained on my back for any length of time, or that I seriously expected to be attacked by groundhogs. I suppose I was on my feet again within ten seconds. What really distressed me was the rate at which my fears were multiplying in these unfamiliar surroundings. At any moment, I would trip over an anthill and start reciting from *The Cocktail Party*. I had come out for an enjoyable country ramble, and already it seemed doubtful, unless I took a firm grip of myself, whether I should get any enjoyment out of it at all.

It is not easy to take a grip of yourself when there is nothing to grip *against*. If a pack of wolves had come padding through the trees, I daresay I should have attacked them with almost foolhardy courage. A single puma might have made a man of me. But the silence, the sinister absence of visible life of any kind continued unbroken. I had to fight this thing unaided, with psychological weapons. 'What kind of a fool are you?' I asked myself. 'Do you really imagine you are in any danger, here within five miles of America's most exclusive school?' The answer I gave to that was yes. Very well, then, I argued, go on from there; let your imagination run riot and see where it gets you. Suppose that the worst has happened, and try to visualise the consequences. My family would have to be informed. There would be a cable, sooner or later. I called up a picture of my London home, heard the crunch of the telegraph boy's wheels on the driveway, saw my wife at the door taking the buff envelope from his gauntleted hands. I saw her slit the envelope and take out the flimsy form. 'REGRET TO INFORM YOU YOUR HUSBAND EATEN BY GROUNDHOGS NEAR GROTON. DETAILS FOLLOW. DO YOU WISH REMAINS EXPRESSED TO ENGLAND?

This *reductio-ad-absurdum* method has much to commend it. Make a mockery of one's fear and they dissolve in laughter. I have known it to work with more normal everyday worries. But I overdid it. I got sidetracked on the word 'REMAINS'. I could not help wondering, from what I remembered of Hersey on the voraciousness of groundhogs, whether much – supposing I blundered into a really thick thicket – would be left. Perhaps only the flexible portions of my shoes? It even crossed my mind that I possibly ought to write my name on the soles, for identification purposes.

This was my lowest ebb. There is a pit of abasement that, once reached, practically abolishes fear. A man who has descended to the point of writing on his shoes no longer cares. Thus, in a strangely indirect way, my psychological war was won. I felt that I was not worth saving. We have all got to go sometime, and whether it was to be by way of marmots, from bite of rattlesnake, copperhead, or coachwhip, from fire, poison ivy, heatstroke, or plain exhaustion hardly concerned me now. I turned my back on the river and plunged headlong, caring nothing, into a wall of trifoliate vegetation. Soon the undergrowth thinned and fell away.

In the heart of the forest, the going was easy. Apart from some fallen trees, which I kicked in passing to annoy the fer-de-lances, I met no obstacles. Within ten minutes, I heard a woodpecker call and knew that I must be all but clear of the nature preserve.

Where the sandy track emerged into open fields, I caught a brief glimpse of a groundhog. 'Long, low, brownish,' I wrote in my *Field Guide*. 'Seems scared of Man.' It is the first field note I ever made on groundhogs.

Wild Music

Copywriters ought to think carefully of the possible consequences of their words, and not get innocent third parties immersed in a lot of unwanted cormorants. For instance:

From July through September, the Minack Theatre presents a festival of Greek, Shakespearean, mediaeval, and modern plays. The cry of cormorants and the drum roll of surf add a wild and lonely music.

That is from a recent British Travel Association advertisement in an American magazine, and may well bring shovel-loads of dollar spenders down to the Cornish coast this summer. A good thing for us in Britain and a good thing for the visitors. The Minack Theatre is splendidly set in the open air, and its backcloth of tumbled cliff and wide sea and sky must lend (though I have never had the fortune to be present) an added grandeur to an Oedipus or an Antigone, a Lear or a Lady Macbeth. There can be no objection in principle to an appeal to the people of Omaha and Wisconsin to come over and savour these delights. It is the wild and lonely music I jib at.

I have known the cliffs of Cornwall practically since they were so high. Also their cormorants. These birds (genus *Phalacrocorax*) fly with rapid wing-beats and the keen sense of purpose that an outstretched neck conveys, usually quite low over the open water. They give pleasure by staying longer below the surface when they dive for fish than the watcher can credit, and by reappearing where he is not looking. They stand on rocks and hold their wings out to dry, in a manner that nobody has yet failed to describe as heraldic. But their cry – now, that is a music that I have never yet enjoyed, with or without benefit of surf. One ought to have heard it, I do agree. Stretched out among the sea pinks on Pentire or by Tintagel's legend-haunted steep, one should surely catch, faint and far below, a long, lorn trumpet call, rising and falling, dying yet echoing still – the unmistakable, unforgettable cry of the spume-drenched cormorant. Born of the wind and spray, at one with the magic and mystery of the lonely wastes of water, that poignant, undulating call seems to come to us from some remote past, to carry with it a desolate breath of the days, perhaps fifty million years ago, when *Phalacrocorax* first lived and loved in an Oligocene dawn.

Nature, however, does not always rise to its opportunities, nor does fine writing necessarily make fine birds. The brutal truth is that the cormorant has no cry. It croaks. And even that it only does, as a rule, on its nesting sites. Let us listen for a moment to the authorities, to whose utterances (positively melodious by comparison) I have had recourse in vexation at my inability to recall the living voice of the theatre-haunting cormorant:

It is usually silent away from nesting-sites and roosts, where the chief notes are various deep guttural noises, 'karrk', 'kworrk', etc. – P.A.D. Hollom, *The Popular Handbook of British Birds.*

Rarely heard away from nest, where it has a good many guttural notes. – R.S.R. Fitter, *The Pocket Guide to British Birds.*

Usual note a low, guttural 'r-rah.' – Roger Tory Peterson et al., *A Field Guide to the Birds of Britain and Europe.*

It crossed my mind that the BTA writer, deviating into an error that has trapped others before now, might have mistaken shags for cormorants, perhaps confused by the boom of the surf and some windy mediaeval play. But the same authorities are at least as discouraging about shags:

> Notes at breeding-places are harsh and croaking, recorded as 'kroak-kraik-kroak.' – Hollom.
>
> A harsh croak. – Fitter.
>
> A loud, rasping croak. At nest, a deep grunt and loud hissing. – Peterson.

It becomes uncomfortably clear that Americans are being lured to Minack under something like false pretences. Even if, which I take leave to doubt, there is a cormorant and/or shag nesting colony within croaking distance of the theatre, can one honestly say that wild and lonely music will be provided as advertised? The surf may roll its drums as never before, but what are our transatlantic guests to make of all this guttural grunting and hissing? They might reasonably protest that they could get as good background noises from any London audience – or New York. They might go further and say that they would sooner take their tragedies without interruption. Aeschylus is tricky stuff:

> ORESTES: Oh, heritage of Grief! Incarnate Woe! Oh, bloody hand of Doom that jars the strings! (*Kworrk*) Now is the voice of melody brought low. (*Kwarrk, karrk, kworrk*)
>
> ELECTRA: Oh, how they grate, these harsh chords Sorrow wrings! (*R-rah*)

Even so carefully chosen a passage as that seems doubtfully enhanced to me. Nor can I find in the whole of Shakespeare more than one or two scenes, in *Lear* and *Macbeth*, that could benefit from deep guttural noises *off*, flourish of 'kworrks,' etc. There is a kind of wild and lonely music that just does not go with high tragedy.

Of course, if they were putting on Aristophanes, now, there might be something in it:

CHORUS OF FROGS: *Brekekekex. Koax. Koax.*
DITTO SHAGS (*off*): *Kroak-kraik-kroak.*
BTA COMMENTATOR (*at back*): *Phalacrocorax*!

That should raise a laugh among knowledgeable Chicagoans. Or, rather, it might – but for the sad circumstance that the cormorants and the shags will be through with their nesting by the time the Minack Theatre opens. From July through September, I fear, not a croak will be heard, not a guttural note. The surf will have to go it alone.

The Spy-Ban Pact

1963

The background of the current spy-ban talks is fairly generally known. It would obviously be to the interest of the United States, Great Britain, and the Soviet Union, who have in recent years been compelled to spend crippling sums on their ever-increasing battalions of spies and counter-agents, if agreement could be reached to terminate – or, at any rate, check – the escalating spy race. The difficulties are equally clear. Mutual trust is not to be expected in this field, so that any treaty negotiated must include ample safeguards to ensure that its provisions will be honoured by all signatory powers. Nonetheless, some progress was made, according to informed reports, at yesterday's secret meeting at the Kremlin.

Mr Khrushchev opened the discussion in genial mood by handing to Mr Kennedy forty-eight pages of closely typed foolscap. 'Here,' he exclaimed, 'is a list of American agents known to be operating in the USSR. A full and free exchange of information is the basis of mutual confidence.'

Mr Kennedy took the hint and good-humouredly passed to the Russian leader a three-volume *aide memoire* cataloguing Russian agents operating in the United States, which Mr Khrushchev studied attentively.

At this stage, Mr Macmillan suggested that it might be a good thing if the two lists were compared. Any names occurring in both could then be noted down for withdrawal in the first wave. All parties, he felt sure, would be glad to be rid of their double agents.

'In my country,' observed Mr. Khrushchev, nodding his agreement, 'we have a saying – "The cow that is milked at both ends soon runs dry."'

Mr Kennedy, after a telephone call to his brother in Washington, stated that he was not opposed in principle to the exchange of names. He then made the brilliant, if discouraging, point that the names by which Russian agents were known to the CIA were unlikely to be the same as those by which they were known as American agents to the Russian counter-espionage organisation. The first step, he said, should be to set up a subcommittee of experts to advise on methods of correlating identities. This would avoid confusion. On the question of withdrawal, he thought it right to say, frankly, that he could not guarantee that every agent ordered to cease operations would at once accept the instruction as genuine. It was in the nature of spies to be suspicious.

'Exactly,' Mr Macmillan agreed. 'We have a man up in the Urals – been there for thirty years, off and on – who no longer trusts orders sent from home, or feels it safe to remit classified information back to the government. He is, as we say, spying *in vacuo*, and would be difficult to dislodge.'

'Ah, your Q-7!' cried Mr Khrushchev jovially. 'We know him well. For many years, we have used him as training material for our apprentice counter-agents. If they cannot put the finger on him in three days, they are out.'

There was much laughter at this, which was renewed when Mr Macmillan suggested that this man could be left where he was on some *au pair* arrangement. 'We ourselves,' he admitted, 'would be sorry to lose your Agricultural Attaché. His habit of using crevices in old gateposts—'

Mr Kennedy interrupted to submit that they might be tackling the problem from the wrong angle. A beginning could be made by banning methods rather than men. 'Outlaw invisible ink,' he declared, 'and you have rendered half our agents powerless. Deprive them of number codes, microfilm cameras, hollow shoe heels, and finally money, and the whole ridiculous business would be at an end.' The problem of the agents themselves, which was no easy one, could be dealt with at leisure. 'None of us, I imagine,' he said, 'wishes to be flooded out by a horde of repatriates, many of them unemployable and quite incapable of adjusting themselves to a way of life they have long forgotten. The ultimate disposal of thousands of agents and counter-agents must be a matter for a committee at Ministerial level. It might even be referred to the United Nations.'

Mr Macmillan gave immediate support to the American proposal, but drew attention to the need for adequate supervision by teams of observers to ensure that the agreement was being honoured. 'We cannot undertake to deprive our own men of invisible ink,' he said firmly, 'unless we are assured that Soviet agents are similarly handicapped. Especially in view of the well-known fact that such common materials as lemon juice and milk may be employed as substitutes for invisible ink.'

Mr Khrushchev objected that he could not allow his country to be invaded by bands of uncontrolled foreigners spying on his ink factories and dairy farms, to which Mr Kennedy replied that he thought the Soviet leader was looking at the cart from the wrong end of the horse, if he might make use of a Russian aphorism. It would be in the Soviet's own interest to admit observers. 'After all,' he pointed out, 'they will be there to ensure that *our* spies are deprived of the means of spying.'

Mr Khrushchev is understood to have banged the table at this stage. Trained teams of counter-agents, he declared, already existed in Russia for that very purpose, and he was unable to accept the suggestion that neutral observers would do the job more efficiently than his own men, who were the best in the world. It was an insult to suggest that Russia was incapable of protecting her military secrets without the assistance of contingents of Swedes, Irishmen, and Indonesians.

In the face of this tirade, Mr Kennedy showed his statesmanship by at once conceding the Soviet point. He saw no difficulty at all, he said, if each signatory to the pact were to rely upon its own resources to see that the others were carrying out the terms. The matter could now perhaps be left to a conference at a lower level to draft the precise provisions.

Mr Macmillan said that he was in danger of becoming confused. If the counter-agents of each country were left to ensure that the agents of the co-signatories were unable to operate, he failed at the moment to see how the existing situation would be altered. If, however, the proposal was that the existing situation should *not* be altered, he would certainly be prepared to initial a communiqué along those lines. There would, he thought, be little difficulty in reaching agreement on the precise phrasing, and such a pact, though not perhaps to be described as a breakthrough, would open the door to further profitable discussions with kindred aims. Without wishing to anticipate anything he might say at London Airport on his return, he did not entirely rule out the possibility of an ultimate agreement to do nothing about Berlin.

At this master stroke of international accommodation, the three leaders rose and shook hands. The vodka tray was produced, and Mr Khrushchev, stripping off his coat, offered to take on Mr Kennedy and Mr Macmillan simultaneously at badminton. 'We shall see how good a team you really make,' he said jovially.

The visiting statesmen declined the offer. Mr Macmillan thought it would be wiser to leave the proposal in abeyance, until the preliminaries had been discussed at a lower level. Mr Kennedy, agreeing, said that in any case his sneakers were in his closet, back in Hyannis

Port.

There are strong reasons for believing that the Espionage Status Quo Pact will be signed within the next few days. An argument that is understood to have weighed heavily in its favour with the three statesmen is that it will put France and China in such a devil of a dilemma. As Mr Khrushchev remarked, tossing a shuttlecock from hand to hand, they will either have to endorse it or give up spying.

Pond Life

When my wife leaves me after dinner, as she generally does, to finish my cheese alone, it is my custom to take a book – any book – from our dining-room shelves, open it anywhere, and read. The best cheese palls without a companion. Sometimes I find myself in the middle of an H.G. Wells novel, marvelling at the sheer skill of the man and the neglect into which he has fallen; or it may be a page or two of Somerville and Ross, or Kinglake getting fun out of the plague in Cairo, or a description of the behaviour patterns of the racket-tailed humming-bird, or Chadwick deciphering Linear B, or Henry James weaving and unweaving as tirelessly as any Penelope. There is no order or method about the books in this house, I am glad to say.

I stress the element of chance to show that when I opened Sassoon's *Siegfried's Journey* a few evenings ago it might just as easily (give or take a pound or two) have been Rostovtsev's *Social and Economic History of the Roman Empire*.

Sassoon went on a speaking tour to the United States in 1920, and by page 194, where the book fell open, was in some small difficulty.

> I must explain [he wrote] that my lecture tour had by now become entirely dependent on my ability to obtain engagements by my own exertions. Early in March it had transpired that the Pond Bureau was on the verge of bankruptcy. This had been brought about by the failure of Maeterlinck to speak intelligible English, which had resulted in the cancellation of his tour with a huge loss of money to his agent.

A good Brie, taken in slow mouthfuls between paragraphs, encourages a reflectively sympathetic frame of mind. It was easy to see that Maeterlinck, expounding his mystical symbolism in a language nobody could understand, would test the endurance of the keenest lecturegoer. Bad luck on everyone, not least on Sassoon. Nobody, I should guess, suddenly burst out singing.

Anxious to know more about an agency that thought it could make money out of Maeterlinck, I ate another bit of cheese and hopefully turned back some twenty pages, to the beginnings of Sassoon's chequered trip to the States. There is nothing like aimless research for spinning out a meal, and I was soon rewarded by the discovery that James B. Pond himself, head of the Pond Lyceum Bureau, had come in person to London in the summer of 1919 to renew an invitation to lecture previously made by letter to Sassoon and turned down by him 'owing to inexperience as a public speaker.' Pond, who seems to have had some kind of death wish, pooh-poohed so trivial a handicap, and Sassoon, after trying out his voice in the Albert Hall (a stiffish test that Maeterlinck might have been well advised to copy) eventually set sail for New York some six months later.

'Got off the boat this afternoon about three,' his diary for January 28, 1920, records. 'Met by one of J.B. Pond's people, who brought me to this hotel in a very old taxi through streets inches deep in snow slush. My watch refuses to go, my luggage hasn't yet arrived from the docks, and the hotel is a rather depressing one. I have eaten a nasty dinner. . . .' He had a raging toothache as well. And next morning, calling at the Pond Lyceum Bureau to hear the details of his two months' tour, he 'saw at once that [Pond] was uneasy about something.' No wonder. As far as I can deduce, the Maeterlinck fiasco still lay some weeks ahead, but

By the terms of our agreement he had guaranteed me a minimum of twenty-five lectures at a hundred dollars each, also paying my steamer fares and travelling expenses. It was, therefore, a complete surprise when he glumly announced that only two engagements had been booked for me in February, and none at all in March. He attributed this to the exceptional influx of British authors that winter. . . .

A merry pair they must have been that slushy January morning. But there were no recriminations: 'I was always on the best of terms with Pond, who treated me well. But all he could do was to tell me to collect my earnings independently and pick up what engagements I could as I went along.' Not an easy assignment for a young poet in a strange land, but somehow or other the tour went on, even after bankruptcy had revealed its distressing verge in March. Just how that was achieved I cannot say, for the Brie was finished and coffee would be available elsewhere. I left the table with the conviction that Sassoon was a pretty even-tempered young man and that J.B. Pond, though obviously a likeable chap, had still a good deal to learn about the lecture-tour business.

Imagine my astonishment – but no, on second thought it is too early yet for that. We are coming up to a coincidence, but it must be approached in due order and with proper preparation. It is, then, some three hours later that same evening, and I am settled comfortably in bed, book in hand, ready for my accustomed half-hour read. This is no random volume, opened at haphazard, for at bedtime I read conscientiously, starting at page 1 or earlier. It is, in fact, a biography of H.M. Stanley, written by Byron Farwell, published in 1958, and called *The Man Who Presumed*. I borrowed it about a week ago from the local library, having a weakness for all those intrepid and splendidly quarrelsome explorers whom nothing dismayed except, perhaps, the scepticism of the Royal Geographical Society, and by now my nightly stint of forty or fifty pages had brought me almost to journey's end. Behind lay interminable marches, famine, fever, smallpox, desertions, treachery, Remington rifles and poisoned arrows, drownings, executions, endless recriminations, and occasional moments of triumph. Livingstone had long ago been found and Emin Pasha rescued, neither of them showing excessive delight. Of the six hundred and twenty-three Zanzibaris, sixty-two Sudanese, thirteen Somalis, and ten white men who started out with Stanley on the latter expedition, a total of five hundred and twelve were dead or missing. Stanley had done enough, and I was at liberty, all passion spent, to enjoy Chapter XVII, 'Retirement and Last Days.'

Stanley, I read, married a Miss Dorothy Tennant, who liked to draw ragamuffins and was descended from Oliver Cromwell. And then

On October 29, 1890, the Stanleys sailed for the United States to begin a great lecture tour. . . . Stanley was scheduled to give a hundred and twenty lectures in the United States and Canada. The tour was organized

(I break off here for a moment to allow the reader time to imagine my astonishment)

by Major James B. Pond, who was also booking agent for Mark Twain, Henry George, Bill Nye, and the Ricca Venetian Mandolin Quintette.

James B. Pond, it will be understood, had vanished completely from my consciousness, gone with the Brie, in the three-hour interval since I had first become aware of him, so that this second meeting struck me with astonishing force. Here he was again, thirty years earlier, already hard at it with the Stanleys and the Twains, little dreaming that a generation later, he was to make such an infernal muddle over Maeterlinck and

Sassoon. I could scarcely have been more excited if I had come upon him at Ujiji, wearing a cloth cap and red-sleeved waistcoat, with the blue waters of Lake Tanganyika shimmering in the background.

Stanley was more fortunate than Sassoon in his dealings with J.B., who on this occasion 'had made elaborate plans for his lecturer.' Stanley and his bride, Mr Farwell reports '. . . travelled in a special Pullman car that had been named *Henry M. Stanley*, a grand affair equipped with its own kitchen, a dining room, and a drawing room complete with a piano,' and one cannot help reflecting with a certain sadness on poor Sassoon's very old taxi and depressing hotel. On the evidence, it begins to look as though Pond, the very man who in his heyday had taken Mark Twain *and* the Venetian Mandolin Quintette in his stride, was beginning to lose his touch by the nineteen-twenties.

Or could it be, perhaps, that this was not the same James B. Pond? Americans have a tiresome habit of passing on their first name, initial and all, to their sons, so that a 'Jr' or even a 'II' is sometimes attached for clarity, as they are to yachts and racehorses. And Stanley's Pond was a major, whereas in Sassoon's recollections he is plain Mr – if that. The possibility has to be admitted that what we have here is not one James B. Pond but two, and bang, in that case, goes half the allure of my coincidence. Bang also goes the notion, conceived at about midnight, of writing a definitive Life of James B. Pond, perhaps entitled *From Stanley to Sassoon* – a biography which, as anyone who has had dealings with authors must agree, would have been hardly less replete with interminable journeys, desertions, inability to speak intelligible English, recriminations, and poisoned arrows than Stanley's. If the record shows, as I fear it must, a succession or string of J.B. Ponds, I certainly have no intention of writing a mere brochure about the Lyceum Bureau.

A pity. Still, something remains from my researches between 8 p.m. and midnight. Stanley's greeting to Livingstone is pretty widely known, but how many are aware of *Mrs* Stanley's opening remark to James B. Pond? Here it is, faithfully recorded by Mr Farwell: 'When they were introduced she quietly remarked, "I don't like you, Major Pond."'

This seems to me as memorable in its way as her husband's rather overlauded salute, and it may be that the shock to poor Pond started that decline in his grip on the affairs of the Lyceum Bureau that reached its nadir, thirty years later, with Maeterlinck and Sassoon. Nor can one help reflecting what might have been the long-term results had these two strange greetings of husband and wife been, by some irony of fate, interchanged, had Mrs Stanley very reasonably said, 'Major Pond, I presume?', while Stanley himself (who, after all, only four days before the famous meeting found occasion to carve 'Starving. H.M.S.' on the trunk of a tree) opened up at Ujiji with a brisk 'I do not like you, Dr Livingstone.' For one thing, I suppose, four hundred and forty-five Zanzibaris, fifty Sudanese, twelve Somalis, and five white men might have lived to see Queen Victoria's Diamond Jubilee. But not, perhaps, Stanley.

Autobiographer Manqué

The psychiatrist began his explorations along the accustomed paths, but I soon put a stop to that. 'Do not vex yourself, Doctor,' I said, 'with all this poking and prying into the darker side of infancy. We shall get nowhere with fixations. Your Oedipuses and your ids, your Electras and your Jungs, your Adlers and your Gestalts – let us clear them all, bag and baggage, out of this conversation. It happens, you see, that I know the cause of my present state of acute melancholia.'

'Indeed!' he said, permitting himself the unlovely smile of a psychiatrist who has heard a similar claim before.

'Yes. From the age of six—'

'You propose to tell me the story of your life?'

'Exactly, if by "life" you mean Life. You have, I suppose, in your leisure hours, read some lives, letters, memoirs, and autobiographies?'

'Of course. In one's endless search for a deeper understanding of the ego—'

'Good. Then you may be able to appreciate to some degree the frustrations I have had to endure. Any man with the desire to write his memoirs—'

'You desire to write your memoirs?'

'Naturally.'

'And at what age did you first experience this desire?' he asked, preparing to make a note.

'At six, as I have been trying to tell you. It was, as I recall, on the morning of my sixth birthday that the revelation came to me. I was patted on the head by a neighbour, whose name I forget—'

'Hard?'

'What do you mean, hard?'

'Was it a hard pat?'

'Soft to medium. I felt no after effects, other than distaste. "And what", this old gentleman asked me, "are you going to do when you grow up, my boy?" – to which I replied without hesitation, "I am going to write my memoirs," and from that resolve I have never faltered.'

'I see. You were born, I take it, into a poor and underprivileged home, and your earliest recollection is, perhaps, of the jet-black beads on your mother's faded bonnet?'

'My mother never wore a bonnet. I spoke to her sharply about that, in or around the month of January, 1913. "What is the use to me," I said, "of the utterly unmemorable clothes you consistently wear? Nothing trails or jingles. My father is just as bad. Here you both are – nice, kind, affectionate parents with a sufficiency of means, living in a comfortable, well-ordered home, with not so much as a backhanded blow from the warming pan or a paragraph's worth of traumatic obscenities between you." I had mastered the language, you see, before my seventh birthday; it was the material that was lacking. "Why can't my daddy come home roaring drunk every Saturday night," I demanded, choking back my tears, "or at least waste his substance on some ludicrous hobby like collecting horse brasses? And where are the eccentric uncles and aunts that any dedicated autobiographer has a right to expect? Two dull bankers and an Aunt Sybil, who never threw a fit or attacked a clergyman with an umbrella in her life!"'

'There were compensations, surely?' the psychiatrist suggested. 'You had a lovable nanny, I do not doubt, full of quaint aphorisms and to this day, at the ripe old age of eighty-six, a cherished repository of childhood memories.'

'We shall get on a great deal faster if you will allow

me to tell my story in my own way. Suffice it to say that, leafing through my journal in my tenth year, I could find nothing more worthy of publication than a fall of soot at the Vicarage in the winter of '16 and a runaway horse stopped, within twenty yards, by a man called Heathers. You may imagine with what eagerness I looked forward to my departure from this barren Elysium for a boarding school in Kent. There, as my extensive reading told me, I should be miserably unhappy. Bullied and despised, longing in vain for privacy, the leaves ripped wantonly from my favourite copy of Virgil, I should hug to my lonely breast a rich and ever-growing store of memorable resentments. Add to that the possibility, with luck, of a few unsavoury incidents and all the disastrous upheavals of puberty, and you see why I set off with the highest hopes and a woolly bear deliberately displayed among my luggage to excite derision.'

'And?' he put in, shooting an expectant glance over his spectacles.

'I enjoyed every minute of it. Top of the class at almost every stage of my educational career, I might at least have earned some sneering shouts of "Beastly swot!" but I had the misfortune to be hopelessly good at games into the bargain and accordingly suffered from a high degree of unreadable popularity. I ended my school days with about two dozen silver cups and a shelf of irreproachable books bound in half-calf. Not a usable paragraph among the lot. You cannot make a silk purse out of half-calf. I was not even struck down during my adolescence by one of those lingering and near-fatal illnesses out of which so many a chapter of half-caught whispers, gently undulating curtains, intimations of mortality, and semi-conscious maunderings has been constructed by more fortunate writers.'

'You proceeded, of course, to Oxford?'

'Inevitably, yes.'

'That would be, let me see, in the twenties, would it not – that golden age when such rare spirits as Evelyn Waugh and Harold Acton transmuted the most mundane events into precious metal. Entrancing cups of tea with Father Ronald Knox, long unforgettable evenings while the claret circulated and Maurice Bowra and John Betjeman—'

'Never met any of them. Strange as it may seem to you, who have clearly read as many memoirs as the next man, I did not even know they were there. Out of the dozens – I might even say the scores – of friends I made, not one enriched my journal with a quotable epigram or possessed a name that could with advantage be dropped into an index. Once only, I remember, did I believe myself to be upon the verge of a bit of copy, when a man called Smith, or Smithers, but otherwise unremarkable, rolled up his sleeve one lovely May morning, as the sunlight glittered and danced upon the waters of the Cherwell and from every tower and spire the chiming bells seemed to re-echo a cascading obbligato to the yearning thoughts, the heartache, and the pain—'

'Yes, yes.'

'Forgive an old man his dreams. It was half past eleven, to cut a lot of chiming short, and this chap Smithers, or Smithson, was trying to fish out of the water a pewter tankard that he had inadvertently dropped, when I chanced to see upon his forearm the telltale pinpricks—'

'Heroin? Cocaine?'

'Neither. Apparently the man had fallen into a bramble bush while out beagling. Everything I touched turned to literary dross. Nothing that glittered was golden – not even this man's arm. And it was no better when, with renewed hope, I left my alma mater's sheltering walls, its smooth lawns and sequestered groves, and found myself pitchforked – metaphorically, of course, – into the great bustling world ouside. Now was the time for me to be "taken up", to my delighted surprise, by the good and great. Lady Astor would ask me to tea. Max Beerbohm, Lady Cunard, and, I need hardly add, Lady Ottoline Morrell would insist on my shy attendance at soirées, where the talk would fizz and sparkle like the pink champagne served by kindly old butlers. Actresses, statesmen, poets, judges would litter the pages of my journal. "Luncheon with Augustus John," I should note. "On to Ellen Terry's, where Bertrand Russell had a good story about H.R.H. Beaten at bezique by Winston." Reality once again let me down. These people were all either dead or unaware of my youthful promise.'

On his pad the psychiatrist was making a drawing, which looked, from where I sat, like a fir tree with an inverted bucket on top.

'Though I did once,' I went on, raising my voice, 'see Stanley Baldwin at a club, drinking soup.'

'What happened?'

'He had a chop to follow.'

'And then?'

'Cheese.'

'I see.'

He initiated those small movements – a squaring up of papers, an uncrossing of the legs – that mean one's three-quarters of an hour are nearly over. 'To recapitulate then,' he said, 'you have led a totally undistinguished life, unenriched by eccentric relatives, misery at school, Evelyn at Oxford, or even acquaintanceships scraped in latter life with household names, and you feel inhibited by these disadvantages from writing the memoirs that, from an early age, it has been your ambition to produce. You have become aware, to put it bluntly, that insignificance cannot effectively be chronicled. Is that an adequate summary?'

'Well, now—' I began.

'Your case is in many respects unique. Would to God

that it were not so. It only remains for me to thank you, on behalf of the reading public, for your unparalleled restraint and self-denial, and to say that the least I can do under the circumstances is to remit my customary fee.'

I thought that very kind. I left him, as one does after unburdening oneself to an understanding listener, in a much calmer and more contented frame of mind. Indeed, such was my euphoria that no task, however difficult, not even the writing of my memoirs, seemed beyond my powers. The least I can do, should this mood persist, will be to send the psychiatrist a copy.

On the Left as You Enter

A point about church guides, not perhaps immediately apparent to those who buy them, is that they do not write themselves. By 'church guides' I mean those small booklets to be found in many parish churches, in a wooden holder on a table near the font, surmounted by a request to put two shillings in the box by the south door. Their aim, apart from a useful reinforcement of the fabric fund, is of course to give the visitor some account of the age and history of the building, to draw his attention to beauties and curiosities he might otherwise miss, and to send him on his way with an illustrated memento of his visit which, for years afterwards, he neither knows where to put nor quite likes to destroy. A subsidiary function of many guides is to pay tribute to benefactors, notably 'Sir Hugo and Lady B. . . , by whose generous aid the fifteenth-century screen was recently restored and regilded.'

Guides are written in a special language of their own. Not only church guides but guides of all kinds: borough guides, brochures about stately homes, pamphlets on Lake Como issued by travel agents – all have a uniformity of style that suggests they were written by machine, or perhaps by pupils of some great Central college of Guide-writing where the principles of exposition are laid down in a correspondence course of twenty-six lessons. There is a liking for the passive voice. 'From the top of the Tower (late XIVth cent) wide views of the surrounding countryside may be obtained.' 'Access to the Crypt is to be had on application to the Sacristan (Mons & Fris).' 'Leaving the building by the side door' (what we used to call the *nominativus pendens* at school is widely approved in guiding circles), 'a massive column is to be observed.'

Not always the passive voice though. Sometimes what can only be called the personal or contiguous mood breaks in. The writer joins the party, takes them by the hand and leads them companionably from pillar to post, from aisle to apse. 'After viewing the tomb of Sir Nicholas ffulke, on which we note the curious beehive motif, we pass at once into the Chancel, greatly enlarged in 1870.' This comparatively cosy approach seems, as far as my reading goes, to be reserved for buildings and is not recommended for local or borough guides. The latter never, I believe, go so far in familiarity as to point out that 'after a dip in the commodious Public Baths (closed on Tuesdays) we can enjoy a game on the Putting Green (3s) or a ramble along the Promenade', preferring the more distant 'The visitor will find within easy reach', or the classic 'Ample facilities for recreation are available in the neighbourhood.'

It begins to look as though correspondence courses for guide-writers must be subdivided according to the subject of the guide desired, with a list of do's and don'ts appropriate to each. It would never do, for instance, for the writer of a church guide to dismiss the eighteenth-century pews with an offhand 'Ample facilities for worship are available in the nave'. We may yet have to ask ourselves whether the writing of guide-books is quite as mechanical an exercise as at first appeared.

It isn't. I can say this with all the assurance of one who not long ago undertook the writing, or more accurately the rewriting, of a small brochure about his own parish church. 'By all means,' I answered confidently when approached, and thumbed with disdain through the outdated hotchpotch that has served as a guide for the last forty years.

The first snag lies in the author's determination to be different. Not for him the ritual language, the passives, the slow progression up nave and aisles, the tedious paragraphs about forgotten bones and '. . . that same Elizabeth Amelia Trench, with whose tragic story we have already been rendered familiar by a finely lettered brass plaque (left of South Door, as you enter)'. No wide views from the tower commanded here. This is to be such a guide as never yet was written: simple and informative, but shot through with enthusiasm; stylish but not mannered; orderly, yet aglow with life and movement; an evocation, in a dozen pages or so, of all that this ancient church has seen and been and meant to generation after generation of parishioners since King John rode to Runnymede. The pair of silk bookmarkers kindly presented by Miss Phyllis Arundel in 1906 will have to go. Such, in brief, is the author's modest plan. How to set about it, exactly?

A second embarrassment likely to hold up completion, or even inception, of the work is on the score of accuracy. The old guide is full enough of facts, categorical about dates and architectural styles – replete, heaven knows, with footnotes and addenda by later hands. But it is short on sources. Suppose the old vicar who started the ball rolling in the 1890s chanced his arm and cut a few corners? It is impossible to set about re-using this material, in however superior and cliché-free a style, without questioning one's right to risk the perpetuation of errors. Somebody knowledgeable might walk in one day and flatly state that the pulpit was not mid-eighteenth-century, as described, but a patent Victorian copy. It could even be Sir John Betjeman, doing a TV programme, so that national would be added to local shame.

One can always check with Pevsner, of course; but he, though he mentions a great deal, cannot mention everything. He does not, for instance, mention our pulpit.

The author, whose original assignment was simply to rewrite the old brochure, finds himself forced willy-nilly into research. Helpful people in the village make casual reference to the parish records, to the county archives, to the proceedings of the local historical and archaeological society. It is almost as difficult to admit that one had no thought of setting foot in these quagmires as it is to get out of them, once in. The kindness of the secretary of the archaeological society to whom I applied for a glance at the proceedings sucked me into a bottomless pit of confusion. He thought I might like to look at their collection of church drawings by John Buckler, which would almost certainly include our own church. I looked, it did, and I was astounded.

The parapet along the top of the outer wall of the south aisle was added in the sixteenth century, when the south porch was built. The old guide says so, categorically, and notes for good measure that the parapet was 'renovated' in 1876. John Buckler's drawing, done in 1839, revealed no trace of any parapet on the south wall, but only on the porch; and when I pointed out this surprising omission to the secretary he swiftly produced another drawing of the church, made by W.W. Wheatley ten years later, also parapetless. What became of our parapet, some time between the reigns of Henry VIII and Queen Victoria? And how do you renovate a parapet that is not there? Was it never there? Or did Buckler somehow fail to see it, and Wheatley perpetuate the error (grim omen!) by simply copying Buckler instead of going back to source?

The attempt to resolve this anomaly drove me to the churchwarden's accounts in the county record office, where I became lost for hours in spidery seventeenth-century entries about shoes for Jno Hicks and 'ale fr ye Ringers 4d', finally emerging clueless by that same door wherein I went. There comes a time when every man must decide for himself whether to spend the rest of his life in the Muniment Room of the British Museum or cut all mention of parapets out of his brochure and get the job done. It is not so easy a decision as you might think, once the lust for original research is aroused.

A third snag, in addition to the desire to be different and the fear of perpetuating error, is the risk of giving offence. Suppose that same Phyllis Arundel, whose book-markers we have already determined to excise, turned from good works to marriage in 1908 and became the grandmother of the present verger?

I do not for a moment wish to deter anyone who may be thinking of rewriting a church guide from undertaking the task. It is on the whole an enjoyable occupation. There are, I only wish to state, certain pressures; and these result, in my experience, in a new guide indistinguishable from any other guide that ever was written. But the process of producing that result, whatever else it may be, is not mechanical.

Shadows Over Syracuse

1979

It may seem ungracious, at this centenary of his death, to ventilate a grievance against the Rev Francis Kilvert, but the fact is that it would have saved me a great deal of trouble if the gentle diarist had not gone for a walk across the Doldowlod suspension bridge with a Mr Venables on Wednesday 28 September 1870.

Francis Kilvert, as anybody knows who has read or heard of his journals, was a curate at Clyro in Radnorshire at this time and set down many curious and sensitive observations about people and places; so it was natural that when Venables happened to mention in the course of their walk that he had had tea with Wordsworth at Rydal Mount, Kilvert should make a note of it. Having tea with Wordsworth at Rydal Mount was one of the experiences (like paying a visit to Thomas Hardy in later years) that nobody who aimed to command attention in speech or writing could afford to be without. So Venables told Kilvert, and Kilvert wrote it down.

No harm in that. But Venables, not content with tea, met Wordsworth a second time, and made no secret of the fact. At some point during this same visit of his to Ambleside, and after the tea-party, Venables went for a ride and by chance – so he said – he '... saw Wordsworth sauntering towards me wearing a shade over his eyes, which were weak, and crooning out aloud some lines of a poem which he was composing.' Venables apologised for the accidental intrusion on this bardic exercise, but Wordsworth was gracious and the following notable exchanges then occurred:

'He said' (this is quoted from Kilvert's *Diary* quoting Venables on what the poet said, and calls strictly speaking for an absolute proliferation of inverted commas, but anyway—)

'He said, "I am glad I met you for I want to consult you about some lines I am composing in which I want to make the shadow of Etna fall across Syracuse, the mountain being some forty miles from the city. Would this be possible?" I replied that there was nothing in the distance to prevent the shadow of the mountain falling across the city. The only difficulty was that Etna is exactly due north of Syracuse. "Surely", said Wordsworth, "it is a little north-east or north-west?" And as he was evidently determined to make the shadow fall the way he wanted it I did not contradict him.'

There, grievously, the record ends, leaving unendurable gaps. If Venables went on to answer any of the questions that leap automatically to an inquiring mind, Kilvert does not trouble to mention it. If Kilvert went straight home to his library to check up on Venables' rather over-confident geography, he omits the circumstance from his *Diary*.

What can scarcely be doubted is that Wordsworth strode back to Rydal Mount in something of a tizzy and took it out on Mrs Wordsworth. It is not difficult, without the aid of a Kilvert or a Venables, to reconstruct the scene:

MRS W: Did you have a nice walk, William?

MR W: (*starting up from his atlas*) I have been considerably incensed. That man Venables, whom I encountered by chance while composing some lines on Sicily, attempted to convince me that Mount Etna lies due north of Syracuse.

MRS W: How provoking!

MR W: I make it some eighteen degrees west of true North. What is the maximum northing of the Sun at the summer solstice in Latitude 37 N?

MRS W: Well now, let me see—

MR W: It is intolerable that I should be debarred by a

mere accident of geography from letting Etna's shadow fall on Syracuse. 'When Etna's shadow falls on Syracuse' is a perfect example of the felicity with which a poetic thought may be expressed in the language of everyday. What would have become of Xanadu, if some pedant on horseback—

MRS W: Take no notice, dear. Don't you remember that, in your Preface to 'An Evening Walk: Lines Addressed to a Young Lady', you wrote of your 'unwillingness to submit the poetic spirit to the chains of fact and real circumstance'?

MR W: Yes, yes, that is all very well. I have acquired since then a considerable reputation for accurate measurement, as with ponds.

MRS W: Of course, if Etna happened to be in eruption, perhaps the pall—

MR W: (*coldly*): Out of the question! Streams of molten lava have no place in the lyric of shady contentment I have in contemplation. I will not make shadows out of cinders to please Mr Venables. . . .

So what next?

Dorothy could have told him what to do. She gave him eyes, she gave him ears, she gave him all his best ideas. In the old Alfoxden days she would have seen straight through to a solution of her brother's difficulty:

DOROTHY W: If you want to write 'When Etna's shadow falls on Syracuse', go ahead and write it, William. All you have to do is to turn it into a non-event, one of the never-nevers like snowing ink or Birnam Wood coming to Dunsinane –

> And Christians shall be reconciled with Jews
> When Etna's shadow falls on Syracuse

You see what I mean?

MRS W: Oh *yes*. You could do absolutely anything with

geography like that. 'When Afric's shores are laved by China seas' would be nice. Or you could make Helvellyn tower o'er Everest.

MR W: This is no laughing matter, Mrs Wordsworth. . . .

But Dorothy, alas, was no longer, at the time of Venables' visit, capable of helping. Her sad degeneration had begun. Venables said as much to Kilvert when describing the tea-party. 'Wordsworth's sister Dorothy was in the room, an old woman at the time. She was depressed and took no part in the conversation and no notice of what was passing.' Wordsworth had to worry it out alone. And my personal view is that his inclination would be to tackle the thing head on: to sit down at his desk, scribble at the top of a sheet of paper 'Lines Composed at Rydal Mount after a Chance Encounter with an Acquaintance who sought to convince the Author that Mt Etna bears due North from Syracuse', and plunge right in with

Venables! When, with compass and protractor,
You sought to cabin my Sicilian muse. . . .

That is what I should have thought he would have done. But did he? It is a remarkable fact that neither Venables, as recorded by Kilvert, nor Kilvert in his own right as diarist, expresses the faintest curiosity as to whether Wordsworth did actually, by whatever means, contrive to make Etna's shadow fall where he wanted it to. The huge literary question mark is left suspended in the air.

So it was up to me.

To read right through the collected works of William Wordsworth looking for Syracuse is a task from which I should not flinch, if called upon. I have in my time read clean through Shelley in search of paving-stones, after coming upon a 'For Sale' advt in *The Times* offering 'old

Paving Stones associated poet Shelley'. It happens, though, that Venables' mention of Dorothy's condition cuts the work considerably. She became ill in 1829, which means that some six-sevenths of the poet's output is automatically excluded – an acceptable saving. Not to have to run through the 'Prelude', the 'Excursion' and the CXXXII 'Ecclesiastical Sonnets' in a hunt for shadows is a relief to the most passionate researcher. A mere (in my edition) one hundred and twenty-eight pages of close-set versification remain, and I am able to state with certainty that Syracuse, even in full sun, makes no appearance on any of them. Wordsworth gave up; or lacked, at any rate, the nerve to publish.

More than that. He seems to have felt, after the disastrous encounter with Venables, an extreme reluctance to introduce so much as a possible rhyme for Syracuse into the termination of his lines. It is true that in 1830 he rhymed Muse with coos and again with infuse, in 1832 lose with dews, in 1833 Muse and dews in a triple rhyme with refuse, while in 1834, refuse is coupled with abuse. This inclines me to date the meeting with Venables in the latter part of 1834, after which 'ooze' rhymes are utterly taboo. (I rightly ignore 'use-abuse' (1839); the words are here used as nouns and rhyme properly speaking with Zeus and juice, not Syracuse.)

He could not face the disappointment. Any termination that reminded him of what he had lost was out. Or perhaps he could not trust himself, if he once composed a line ending, say, in 'views' or 'choose', not to stumble blindly on and fall, like Empedocles, into Etna. Think what it must have cost him! A man who is hard pressed – and during this later period Wordsworth went as far afield in his search for rhymes as knees and St Bees, skiff and Hippogriff, Colyseum and Te Deum, even cell and intangible – does not lightly cast away the opportunities afforded by hues and blues, by news, mews, peruse, shoes, Toulouse, and twenty more. He would have none of them. For over a dozen years, through rather more than two thousand, six hundred and forty rhymed lines, until the pen finally fell from his ageing fingers in 1847, he resolutely set aside the temptations of crews in trews, long queues for pews, woos against a background of yews, cockatoos in zoos, booze or (better) brews in the widow's cruse, stews, Waterloos, canoes and kangaroos (whose?)

The wound went deep. The loss to literature is serious. I rate Venables not far behind the Man from Porlock as a murderer of memorable lines from the Lake Poets.

Of course, to put beyond all doubt my case for Wordsworth's horror of rhymes to Syracuse in the post-Venables period, it would be necessary to prove his fondness for them in earlier years by counting their incidence in the remaining six-sevenths of his work. But there are dangers in an over-indulgence in Wordsworth's company. The poet himself has said so. 'Her brother told me' – this is Venables again, via Kilvert, contributing a final tea-time recollection on the subject of poor Dorothy – 'Her brother told me he attributed the failure of her health and intellect to the long walks she used to take with him.'

Yes indeed.

Sense and Centenaries

(1975. Written to commemorate the bicentenary of Jane Austen's birth)

That Sir Walter Elliott, of Kellynch Hall, in Somersetshire, should never rest his eye upon any other entry in *Who Was Who* than his own is not to be supposed.

'I never thought highly of Ellenborough', he had been heard to observe to his elder daughter Elizabeth; 'your attorneys too readily engage themselves in the affairs of others to be altogether gentleman-like.'

On a different occasion a fitful draught so far disturbed his choice of reading that he found himself contemplating, with wrinkled lip, the careers of several Elphinstones, until a sense of what was owing to himself restored his attention to a more familiar and more welcome creation.

No such predispositions, however, confined the enjoyment of his younger daughter Anne. *She* did not scruple to turn the pages of the great book as fancy or inclination dictated, nor did she feel herself ill-used if it fell open as far afield as Lord Acton or the Bishop of Zululand. It was Anne who, on receiving the volume from Sir Walter when he had satisfied himself with a third or fourth reading of his own history, quietly withdrew her eyes from a page that, through her father's self-indulgence, had long excited her disgust and was soon agreeably refreshing her jaded spirits with other names, other histories.

Experience had taught Anne that sensible conversation, a sympathetic concern with people, problems, the world that lay outside his own narrow circle of acquaintance, were not to be expected from her father or Elizabeth. But now, as she bent her head over the pages, she made a discovery which her lively mind and generous wish to please prompted her, despite every discouragement, to share with her companions.

'Austen, Jane,' cried Anne. 'Born December the 16th, 1775. No very prolonged reflection is needed to convince me that she would have been two hundred years old this Christmas.'

'Austen?' replied Sir Walter with a shrug. 'I have no one of my acquaintance with that name. There was at one time a Sir Austen, I believe, who dabbled in the offensive trade of politics.'

'Did not his father Joseph manufacture screws in Birmingham?' put in Elizabeth coolly.

Anne was not to be so easily put down by their ill-bred disdain.

'You do not entirely comprehend me,' said she. 'The lady who at present commands my interest is a Miss Austen, the daughter of a respectable clergyman, of Steventon in the county of Hampshire. Do not you know that she is the author of some six or seven romances praised on every hand for their neatness of xpression, propriety of diction and refined delineation of character?'

'Novels!' rejoined Sir Walter, looking his indignation. 'I am by no means disposed to countenance the mention in my house of so objectionable a mode of writing. Romances,' turning to Elizabeth, 'as your sister presumes to call them, excite my contempt on a number of counts. In the first place—'

Whatever were the grounds upon which Sir Walter based his dismissal of Miss Austen's pretensions, they were not now to be heard. The sound of wheels on the gravel, followed soon after by the announcement of a party of callers, brought his opening periods abruptly to a conclusion and he retired to a far corner of the room in no more contented a frame of mind than is commonly the lot of persons who, with nothing of consequence to say, feel all the mortification and indignity of being deprived of an opportunity to say it.

Their unexpected visitors proved, to Anne's pleasure at least, to be all old friends, and in the bustle and animation of arrival, greeting exchanged, inquiries to be made, every body delighted, nothing so agreeable as a surprise, Anne had time only to observe that the party included Mr Knightley, Miss Bates, Mr Woodhouse and his daughter Emma, Frank Churchill, Mr Bennet with *his* daughter Elizabeth, Mr Collins, Mr Henry Dashwood and the Misses Dashwood, Mrs Norris, Mr Edmund Bertram looking grave, General Tilney, and Miss Mary Crawford with a number of young men in attendance, before her attention was claimed by Mrs Elton, who pushed herself forward with—

'Is not this a good scheme? My brother's barouche-landau – my brother, Mr Suckling of Maple Grove, you know – happened to be not required and it was very soon spoken for, I assure you. "Let us make a plan," said I. Mr Bennet heard me. "Let us make up a party," I said – Did not I, Mr Bennett? "Let us all call upon Sir Walter and family, to wish them the compliments of the season," I said. And here we are! Was not that well thought of?'

'You must have been a little crushed, I fear.'

'Oh no, indeed. My brother's barouche-landau—'

'Mrs Elton is not easily crushed,' said Mr Bennet.

Anne could not but be reminded, by Mrs Elton's alluding to the season of the year, of the subject that had so lately engaged her attention and aroused her compassionate reflections upon the passage of time. A pause in the flow of talk at length afforded an opportunity, long sought after, to share her discovery with a mind of more solid worth, of very much more real understanding than her father's.

'I have been reading,' turning eagerly to Mr Bennet, 'of Miss Austen, of Miss Jane Austen of Steventon in the county of Hampshire. It is her anniversary, you know. Is it not strange? She was to be two hundred this very month.'

'You had better not let Sir Walter hear of it. Age distresses him.'

'Oh, as to centenaries and every thing of that kind, I declare I have no patience,' cried Mrs Elton. 'It does not signify to *me* whether a person is two hundred or a hundred and ninety-nine. Only think! If we had all been born with eight fingers and toes instead of ten, should we not then be celebrating Miss Austen's anniversary in—I do not clearly comprehend *when* we should be doing so. Mr E will tell us.'

Mr Elton looked his ability to help, but said nothing.

'Very true. That is very true, Mrs Elton,' said Mr Weston, who had just now joined the little group with Emma upon his arm. 'We must all be thankful indeed that providence has equipped us to count so comfortably in round numbers. The fowls of the air, I believe, who have but four or five toes, are quite without the means of enumerating even the eggs within their nests.'

Emma had time to observe that Mr Knightley, standing a little apart, had turned away to hide his contempt of such folly, before interposing a sensible reminder that the movements of the heavenly bodies were themselves not without influence on the passing of the years. 'Were the earth to complete her journey round the sun in no more than a hundred and eighty days, we should all be twice as old as we are now. Do not you agree, Anne?

Whatever may have been Anne's opinions on an observation that struck her with all the force of novelty, they were not to be granted the opportunity of expression. Her father, who had for some time been listening to the interchange with a countenance of growing disapprobation, now broke out angrily, 'I am by no means disposed to agree that the movement of any thing has power to affect the age or, I presume to add, the looks of any body with a proper regard for his appearance. There may be those' – with a conscious glance at Lady Catherine de Bourgh – 'for whom, I am ready to believe, the years pass more rapidly than for others who have been, I will not say more fortunate but less exposed to the disgusting ravages of time.'

All felt the impropriety, the loss of ease. All *wished* for something to say, but all lacked the power of utterance. Emma herself, with a determination to share with Mr Knightley some reflections on the evil of consequence unsupported by sound judgment and the insensibility – worse, the indelicacy to which vanity corrupted by defective principles could lead, had at last composed herself to begin when Miss Bates was heard to say:

'Journeys round the sun, did somebody say? I am sure I do not quite understand – Everyone so clever! And Miss Austen too! I said to Mr Darcy, did not I, Jane? "Mr Darcy", I said, "is not Miss Jane" – that is the other Miss Jane, not Miss Fairfax, of course, "Miss Jane Austen", I said, "is not she clever, though perhaps not always very – Such disagreeable ladies as she tells of – I don't think I ever!" Oh, there you are, Mrs Norris! *And* Miss Elizabeth Elliott! How do you do? Mrs John Dashwood, too, and is that dear Mrs Elton? Delightful. Such a brilliant company! Where was I? Oh yes, I was remarking on Miss Austen's disagreeable ladies, dear Lady Catherine.'

'This will never do,' said Mr Knightley, taking Emma aside. 'This is worse than anything. Not to be borne! Will no one put a term to her imprudence? Let Miss Bates be taken into the garden. Half an hour in the shrubbery might tranquillise her.'

Mr Woodhouse, whose hearing was rarely at fault when a lady's walking without doors was proposed, began to be very agitated. 'I should not at all recommend Miss Bates to venture upon any such thing,' said he. 'It is very damp.'

Miss Bates, with rather more animation and fewer digressions than in present circumstances some of the company could wish, was continuing her catalogue of Miss Austen's insufferable women, had disposed of Mrs Clay and plainly was searching her memory for the names of Lucy Steele and Mrs Ferrars when an interruption occurred from an unexpected quarter.

'Come, Miss Bates,' cried Admiral Croft in his hearty way. 'Let us be fair to Miss Austen. Her women, I grant you, are often of such a character, so uncharitable, so offensive an admixture of condescension and impertinence, so lacking in amiability, and in some cases so deficient, I regret to say, even in delicacy and moral principle that one would be reluctant, *more* than reluctant to admit them to one's acquaintance. That much I grant you, Miss Bates. But what of her men? Do not you agree that a finer collection of snobs, bores and sanctimonious prigs was never yet gathered together within the pages of some half-a-dozen books?'

A murmured 'Hear! Hear!' from a corner of the room where Mr Wickham, Mr Willoughby, Mr Henry Crawford and Mr Walter Elliott had been for some time conversing quietly together did no more than momentarily check the Admiral's course.

'Ay, and more than that,' he continued warmly. 'For selfishness and rascally folly, for dissipation, unscrupulous trifling, black ingratitude, avarice, indulgence and duplicity, for downright treachery and, I do not hesitate to add, sheer moral turpitude, where shall we look to find the equal of some of Miss Austen's younger men?'

'And she a clergyman's daughter!' whispered Fanny Price to Mr Collins. 'Is it possible?'

'Upon my word, you express your opinion very decidedly,' said Sir Thomas Bertram, with all the advantage of a man lately returned from Antigua. 'Yet I venture to say that, far removed though many of Miss Austen's characters may be from that right judgment, those sound principles of conduct for which we look in our own families, our own acquaintance, there never was, I believe, a gathering of persons in whose company' – with an amiable glance around the room – 'any one of us would prefer to pass a quiet afternoon or evening.'

His younger son Edmund looked grave, and Mr Edward Ferrars began to feel the need of an interval of meditation, of serious reflection. But a hearty 'Well said!' from Frank Churchill and an equally warm '*There* is her art! *There* is genius' from Captain Benwick more exactly reflected the general complaisance with Sir Thomas's verdict.

Captain Harville, who had hitherto confined himself, with unaffected benevolence, to an occasional nod of agreement with what was going forward, now had a proposal to make. 'On this occasion and at this season,' said he, 'would not it be appropriate, if Sir Walter will so far indulge us and if, as I believe to be true, good Mrs Weston did not neglect to include one or two bottles—'

'An excellent scheme, my dear Harville,' cried Mrs Elton. 'The hamper is in the barouche-landau. Fetch it quickly, Mr E!'

There was general assent, glasses procured with alacrity, warm congratulations for Captain Harville, nobody could have thought of it, only to be expected from one whose profession called constantly for swift decision, bold expedients. Mr Woodhouse's approval of the plan, however had still to be obtained, and many anxious faces were turned in his direction until he was heard to say—

'I do not think that a small glass of Mr Weston's good wine, sipped slowly with a little water, would be unwholesome. By all means let us drink to the memory of poor Miss Austen.'

'Why "poor", papa?' said Emma, smiling. 'She never married, you know.'

All felt the impropriety, but all drank.

Was Blücher Late at Marathon?

It was before the invention of the wheel. Sun worship went on, involving the sacrifice of blondes in bras and primeval minis. Cremation was practised, the body, dead or alive, being pushed out to sea on a raft. Husbandry was primitive. These appeared to be a Mesolithic people, living on fish, fruit, and the flesh of saurians. Oil of a thick, yellowish kind, was employed to set fire to a diplodocus (or perhaps an iguanodont), which came adrift from its halter and threatened mountainous havoc. The moon had not yet been born, though the sun was clearly in labour and flashed prodigiously. When parturition eventually took place, man, after some momentary confusion, took the new orb in his stride. Its phases were chalked up on the rocks, and calendar-making began. The first full tide was for some reason a good deal delayed, but when it came it was a whopper. None of the participants, man or beast, aged at all during the brief span of these catastrophes.

Thus, in short, the scenario of a film called *When Dinosaurs Ruled the Earth.* (Or was it . . . *Roamed the Earth*?) The title was on the screen for less time than the name of the hair stylist, and even that I have forgotten. But as we are about to voyage in some rather strange seas of thought, I think we had better break up the stream of consciousness with a few subtitles of our own e.g.:

REACTION OF AN EDUCATED MAN

The natural reaction of an educated man to this kind of flimflam is scorn. Chronological fiddling, up to a point, is to be expected in a Technicolor excursion into prehistory; anyone who rose up in the balcony and cried out, 'You have blurred the distinction between the Carboniferous and the Permian', would properly be dismissed as a pedant. But to show man shoving stakes into a stegosaurus stretches the credibility gap to something over a hundred and thirty million years, which is too much. The postdating of the birth of the moon by about four aeons is a damned liberty.

WHAT ABOUT ORION, THOUGH?

An educated man intent on nourishing his scorn by checking the approximate dates of terrestrial and celestial epochs is bound to get side-tracked. When, for instance, was Orion born – or, anyway, how far off is it? Well, it turns out that you can't look up the distance to Orion, or to any other constellation. You have to ferret out its individual stars, and the results are highly unsettling. Here is a rundown, at the time of writing, of the distances in light-years of the brightest jewels in Orion's accoutrements: Alnitak, sixteen hundred; Bellatrix, four hundred and seventy; Betelgeuse, five hundred and twenty; Mintaka, fifteen hundred; Rigel, nine hundred; Saiph, twenty-one hundred. Alnilam, plumb in the middle of the belt, is ignored in my table of distances, but I have reason to believe it is about equidistant with Alnitak, give or take a few million million miles. Orion, as viewed, is a fake. Bellatrix is contemporary with Erasmus, and one's view of Rigel, down there at the tip of the sword, was launched during the Battle of Hastings. The whole thing is a worse jumble of periods than the Forum Romanum. And if we turn northward for a glance at the Andromeda Nebula, we are back in the Pliocene era, which is about the gravest disorientation that can occur to the naked eye.

WHITHER IS ALL THIS TENDING?

To a recantation, actually, on a par with Galileo's. Since that vast anachronistic agglomeration we call the night sky is generally accepted as a satisfactory spectacle, worth looking at on a fine evening and strongly suggesting that it has some kind of genuine and contemporaneous existence, it is ridiculous to jib at a few prehistoric blondes being harassed by low-flying pterodactyls. Light is a two-way affair, and if our Jurassic reptiles are now showing on extragalactic screens at around one hundred million light-years away, whil Joan of Arc is clearly and simultaneously visible on Betelgeuse, there is no earthly or universal reason why our own scenarios should not take a broad view. Films like *When Dinosaurs Ruled the Earth* are seen, on reconsideration, to be unnecessarily conservative. We may as well in fact,

DO AS WE WOULD BE DUNNE BY

and draw up a scenario of our own. What I have in mind is a conspectus of world history as viewed simultaneously from various vantage points in the universe – wide-screen stuff, produced by a Toynbee rather than a Joseph E. Levine. When the action opens, it is the Eve of Waterloo, though unlikely to remain so for long.

SCENE: *A gala ball in progress in the Parthenon. Pheidias is putting finishing touches to the decorations. Amid a gay throng of Fourth Dynasty Egyptians, whose profiles are turned to the camera, the tall figure of Wellington, unmistakable in doublet and hose, makes a sombre contrast. He is chatting with Cleopatra and Lady Hamilton, who wear their famous Quatre bras. A distant rumbling is heard without, and Pheidippides gallops up.*

PHEIDIPPIDES: The Fourth Ice Age is advancing! (*Dies of cold.*)

WELLINGTON: Very well. Stand by to repel hordes of

woolly rhinoceroses coming down from the north.

The camera pans, if that is the word, to Samuel Pepys, busy at his electric typewriter. He serves as a sort of continuity man, to keep things in perspective, and has just written (in a manner clearly visible to patrons, even in the cheaper seats). 'Meanwhile, in another part of ye Universe, threatening Magellanic Clouds are gathering.'

A stampede, for the first time on any screen, of woolly rhinos, egged on by Geronimo and quantities of Apaches. It must be realised, as Pepys will explain, that at this time the Thames and the Rhone flowed together into an ocean called Tethys, completely cutting off the US Cavalry from what is now Europe. This obviates any hackneyed situations and raises hopes that the Indians will join Wellington in time.

Enter Edmund Burke at a run, carrying the sacred flame from Olympia. (Or it could be Prometheus, with a badly pecked liver).

BURKE: An event has happened upon which it is difficult to speak, and impossible to be silent.

LADY HAMILTON: (*in some confusion*): Kiss me, Thomas Hardy.

The action now hots up. A group of Neanderthalers, fleeing southward in face of a rumour that their skulls are shortly to be measured, discover the source of the Nile; Archimedes, in a semicomic interlude, tries to invent the wheel, watched by a crowd of jeering Babylonian cyclists.

GENERAL SHERMAN: (*heavily out-numbered at Dismal Swamp by tyrannosaurs, sabre-toothed tigers, etc.*): Where the devil did all these come from?

HARRIET STOWE: I 'spect they just grow'd, like triceratopses.

These events throw Napoleon, whose stagecoach has already been held up by John Wayne, behind schedule, and give an opportunity for a brief dialogue at HQ before the decisive struggle begins.

BENJAMIN FRANKLIN: Easy does it. Little strokes fell great oaks.

GENERAL PATTON: If you believe that, you can believe anything.

Another part of the Acropolis. Enter three Aurignacian blondes pursued by Karl Marx. The Age of Fishes begins – in a small way, at first. La Rochefoucauld gives vent to a suitable aphorism, and a choir of Heavenly voices rouses the Light Brigade to one last assault, reducing the Parthenon to its present state and inflicting an even more far-reaching personal wound.

CLEOPATRA: I'm hit, by God! My nose is half an inch shorter.

WELLINGTON: By God, so it is.

The history of the world changes, to the evident delight of Pascal. The days lengthen perceptibly, and reports of new galaxies pour in as fast as H.G. Wells can log them. It is apparent, as people begin to grope for their hats, that the Universe is contracting again at speeds well in excess of 186,000 miles a second. Queen Victoria, remembering (in a telling flashback) his success over the sparrows in the Crystal Palace, asks Wellington to give his advice in these difficult times. However,

I'D RATHER BE BOILED IN HOYLE, SAYS DUKE

– not very meaningfully perhaps, but it was high time we had another of these subtitles to wind up with.

We Left Out the Fennel

1966

I am looking at a lot of bowls on a broad and spotless surface. They are elegant bowls, of varying sizes, and the surface is, I should guess, heatproof and scratch-proof. There is an oven at right and a woman, centre, behind the bowls. She too is heatproof and scratch-proof, and is shredding borage. She is notably unlike any cook that I have ever seen. It is unthinkable that she should push her hair back from a streaming forehead with the knuckles of a floury hand. She has finished shredding borage, and will tell me later on what to do with it. It is the essence of good, calm cookery to be doing something useful, that will be needed presently, while something else is reaching the stage at which it is needed now.

She has some slivers of fish in one of these bowls and is transferring them to another bowl containing some kind of broth or bouillon, into which she momentarily dips them. She has a way of transferring fish that would surprise a trawlerman. There is in it so much of delicacy and finesse, so sweetly pretty a turning of the wrist as the fillet is caressed by the bouillon, that it is hard to believe that what she has in her hand is a piece of flesh reft from the bones of a lively spotted creature that once undulated on the ocean's sandy floor and waited for its eyes to come uppermost. The contents of the broth we shall remember, she tells me, from last week. That is as it may be. What I shall never understand is why she dips the fish in it. Any possible influence the immersion could have on the fillet, considered as food, must surely be negatived by the much more elaborate mixture or garnish that she is about to spread over and around it before cooking takes place. For this garnish she takes a handful of chopped walnuts, some white wine, not too much fennel, four grapes ('and peel them, please!'), shrimps, mussels, parsley, the yolk of an egg gathered at the full of the moon, half a cup of that damned bouillon, pimentoes, a pinch of curry powder and, of course, some finely kneaded chives. 'Don't forget the chives,' she pleads, giving a swift, neat wipe over that gleaming surface and smiling at me with quick charm, as though to share some housewife's secret: probably the secret is that *I* might well have spilt a little broth, a mussel or two, in all that ferrying to and fro, though she, as it happens, spilt not a drop of anything.

Over all this agglomeration of ingredients she pours a liberal gush of cream, stirs the whole together, and finally engulfs the fish in the rich product, sluicing it over and around the fillets with a kind of figure-of-eight movement of the hand and arm of exquisite precision, and an intimate 'There we are! That wasn't too difficult, was it?'

No indeed. Sprinkle a firkin of grated cheese over the top, my good woman, and pop it in the oven for twenty minutes. At about three hundred and eighty degrees. Or, if cooking by gas—

'Now for the scallops,' she is saying.

I had forgotten that guests were expected. This little pipe-opener that she is demonstrating is a suggestion for a dish my friends will really appreciate, not a few bits of fish, fennel and pimentoes slapped together in a cabman's shelter. Scallops, naturally.

She is wrapping them in bay-leaves and stitching the edges up with what I think may be macaroni. Otherwise, you see, the bay-leaves would uncurl at three hundred and eighty degrees and spoil the surprise. And now we begin to understand the purpose of those filigree baskets, carved out of fried potato, that have been lurking all this time on the extreme edge of the table, almost off-screen. She made them last week and will soon be ready to pop the scallops into them, with a big prawn nestling on top to round the picture. When she has time, she tells me, and wants to make a bit of an impression, she flicks just a touch of silver paint on the prawn's whiskers, immediately before serving.

I can endure this well-meaning woman no longer. She makes a mockery of the genial business of eating. A certain enjoyment of food one must allow. Let fish by all means be served with some kind of sauce. But this is madness. This is civilisation in decay. This is why Rome fell. I am irresistibly reminded, as she prepares to marinate artichokes in a decoction of Marsala and pineapple juice, of the dish called the Shield of Minerva served up for the Emperor Vitellius by his brother and compounded of the brains of pheasants and woodcocks, the sounds of the fish called scari, and the spawn of the lamprey, brought from the Carpathian Sea. It would have fitted easily into this programme. With what untroubled elegance this deft woman would slide the brains of pheasants and woodcocks – 'or', I hear her interjecting, 'if you are in an economical mood, the brains of pigeons will do very well' – into a bowl already frothing and bubbling with the spawn of lampreys bought from a delicatessen shop in Soho, the name of which will be supplied on receipt of a self-addressed, stamped envelope.

I see no hope for Britain. Small wonder that that keen observer, Mr Anthony Lewis, should have written so sadly, some weeks ago, in the *New York Times*, 'The atmosphere in London today can be almost eerie in its relentless frivolousness. There can rarely have been a greater contrast between a country's objective situation and the mood of its people.' Exactly. What are we about that, at a time when 'the pound trembles, the gold runs out, and Britain's ships stand in the dock' (the words are Mr Lewis's, and the ships, of course, are out and about again by now), we should be concerning ourselves with exciting new ways with scallops?

Does this agreeable lady, now shaking something about in a skillet, seriously think that the gnomes of Zurich will be impressed by silver paint on the whiskers of our prawns?

'This is very good,' I said to my wife a couple of days later. 'What is it?'

'It's a TV recipe,' she said. 'You were watching. Only I left out the fennel.'

Make a note of that, Mr Lewis. There are still one or two of us over here who are willing to make some concession to our country's objective situation.

The Trouble with Florence

It is a considerable strain to be about to visit Florence. To revisit Florence must, I think, be purely pleasurable, for then one could sit about in cafés deciding which of its innumerable delights to savour again. A first look at the place has heavier responsibilities, for there must be borne in mind the possibility that it will also be the last look.

The English edition of the Michelin guide to Italy lists under 'Chief Things to See', 'Other Imporant Things to See', and 'Other Things to See' a total requirement of three piazzas, ten churches, five palaces, five museums, two cloisters, two monasteries, and one cathedral, loggia, bridge, garden, and academy each. All these, bearing in mind the readiness with which almost any one of these items subdivides into galleries, chapels, baptisteries★★; campaniles, panoramas, frescoes★★★, tombs★, and sharp instructions to 'note the *Rape of a Sabine* by G. da Bologna (1583),' make a well-laden dish; and while I am labouring under the thought of so much aesthetic pleasure in store, Botticelli suddenly springs to mind.

Botticelli convicts me at once of my personal lack of fitness to visit Florence. I cannot stand his women. The late Dr Thomas Bodkin writes somewhere of 'the power of Botticelli's lovely creatures to entice us into a mood of grace and ease and exquisite fancy.' I must beg, ashamedly, to be excused from any such delicious reverie. His 'graces' are not for me. Of the *Birth of Venus* I can only suppose that the artist had the foresight to realise that it would cut up well for jigsaw puzzles. In *Pallas and the Centaur*, the goddess ('all grace and placid power,' remarks my authority) has precisely that lofty men-are-so-silly expression I used to dread in Paul Jones partners, though none of them carried so huge a halberd. How then am I to conduct myself in the Botticelli Room, when all around me are other tourists in a mood of grace and ease and exquisite fancy? I am hopeless at pretending to be dazed with ecstasy. Standing right in front of the *Hermes* of Praxiteles at Olympia a year or two ago, I tried the expedient of lowering my head, as though in a kind of trance; but I was bothered by a sliver of ham caught between two teeth and could not concentrate. The *Hermes* stands in its own arena of sand as a precaution against damage from earthquakes, which is more than has been done for, say, Nelson's Column, and ought to aid appreciation. But it didn't.

An occasional failure to be ravished by some supreme masterpiece is no great embarrassment in Greece, where there are always plenty of less-trumpeted bits and pieces that one can meet on more relaxed terms and enjoy without compulsion: fragments of sixth-century pediments; river gods exhibiting their muscles in odd corners; vases innumerable, from which it is possible to choose, to say without prompting, 'I like *that* one.' In Florence, my preliminary reading leads me to conclude everything is a masterpiece. 'Florence the Divine,' says Michelin, 'gathers every form of beauty between the hills of the Arno Valley. Idealised by a diaphanous amber light, it mingles art and life gracefully under the sign of the red Turk's-cap lily'. I find that daunting enough, and the names that crop up as one reads further show that there is small chance of resting one's wings, even momentarily, on the second-rate. Everywhere the masters have been at work, and in every known medium. It is not as if you could take a quick overall glance at the outside of some building and then go straight in to get an impression of the height of the Dome***. In all probability Michelangelo has been busy out there, adding world-famous groups of statuary to Brunelleschi's deathless elevation. Donatello will have carved something immortal at the base of the Campanile**. The doorways are certain to be by Ghiberti, with suggestions from Luca della Robbia. Inside, it is a pure toss-up whether the friezes, frescoes, tombs, bas-reliefs, panels, semi-octagonal apses, paintings, medallions, cells, cloisters, pulpits, bronzes, piers, windows, and tapestries are by Raphael, Giotto, Leonardo da Vinci, Fra Angelico, Masaccio, Michelozzo, Michelangelo, Pisano, Jacopo della Quercia, or any conceivable combination of these geniuses. All are unsurpassed, and only a philistine could pass any of them by or fail to gaze up at the Mosaics*** (*Can be lighted by request: fifty lire for five minutes*).

The trouble with Florence is that the moment anybody put up a building, at any time during the fifteenth and sixteenth centuries, a swarm of top-flight artists rushed in with brush and chisel and got to work. They could all do anything. If Michelangelo found that Raphael and da Vinci were already up ladders by the time he got there, he simply threw aside his cartoons and brushes, elbowed Andrea Pisano out of the baptistery, and began to chisel a Madonna. Giotto had probably drawn his last freehand circle by then, but Ghirlandaio and Filippino Lippi would be quarrelling over a window nearby, while Donatello handed over a half-finished figure of Hope to della Robbia and went off to borrow some gold paint from Paolo Uccello. Ghiberti, of course, would be working on doors.

It did not matter a rap to Michelangelo that he was already ten years behindhand on the Pope's tomb; he just could not resist an undecorated building. Nor would the intensity and gaiety of the scene, the din of hammer on chisel, the slosh of wet plaster, the ceaseless rain of wood and marble chips be in the slightest degree lessened if any of the masters I have mentioned happened to be dead or not yet born. There were always plenty of others.

I don't feel fitted to do justice to their combined labours. And even if I take time off from the glories of the past and sit at a café to watch the world go by, my asthetic sensibilities, so I see from a book called *The Land of Italy*, by Jasper More, will still be stretched to the utmost. 'And if the Florentines of the present day,' writes Mr More, 'are no longer the guides and philosophers of Italy, they nevertheless retain a distinction and individuality which immediately strike the visitor. . . . In physical form and beauty the Florentines excel.' The prospect of watching these paragons, at the end of a day of unrelieved masterpieces, makes me thoughtful. The only hope, as far as I can see, is that one or two of my fellow tourists will happen by.

Coming to Terms with the Environment

1971

Years ago, when my own environment was a play-pen, or its Edwardian equivalent, with a couple of small flannel waistcoats airing on one side of it, there was a general belief that every organism had its environment and was affected by it. Moths had one, and became noticeably melanistic if there was a lot of soot about. At this time, too, heredity was a word much bandied about outside the confines of my nursery. Some said that inherited characteristics were more influential and enduring than those developed in and by an individual's surroundings; others said not.

Just when the environment got its definite article I am unable to say. It must have been round about the time that facilities and amenities began to spring up and proliferate in this already overcrowded island. Facilities for recreation, reading, worship, washing and so on took the place of old-fashioned football grounds, libraries, churches etc, and very soon began to group themselves into Amenities by a process akin, it may be, to osmosis. For a man already far gone in middle age it was not easy to adjust to these ameliorations. The concept of adjustment itself was hardly more than embryonic in my formative years. My old nurse, for instance, when she made some irksome change in my environment (a sailor suit, perhaps), never included 'You must learn to adjust to new pressures, Master H' among her innumerable wise saws and encouraging maxims. Still, I made some attempt as time went by to bring order and method, at least in my own mind, into a situation of increasing complexity and actually got to work on the construction of a kind of statistical table, viz.:

Six facilities equal one amenity;
Twelve amenities constitute one planned environment;
Twenty-four planned environments bid fair to attain conurbation status.

If this scheme had gained general acceptance it might have done something to keep the growth of the Environment within bounds. But the idea came too late. In a go-ahead country like ours, where the shilling is dead and the spectre of metrication looms well above the offing, my table had altogether too duodecimal a ring. There was also an infestation at about this time of Neighbourhoods, Precincts (hitherto only encountered in stories about New York cops) and Vertically Integrated Concepts, which were difficult to fit into any comprehensive numerical scheme. Heredity remained reasonably constant, but with the Environment it was becoming daily more arduous to keep in touch. Offshore rigs, to my astonishment, were sunk in it; and to evaluate the influence of these tripods on my characteristics, as compared with my father's genes, was entirely beyond my compass. In my bewilderment I took refuge, I am ashamed to say, in a return to childhood and began to scribble nursery rhymes all over my writing amenities, e.g.:

How many metres to Babylon?
Five thousand six hundred and thirty-one score and ten.
Can I get there by North Sea Gas?
Yes. Facilities for conversion from candlelight are obtainable on application in BLOCK CAPITALS to the
Amenity Controller and his charismatic men.

Meanwhile the Environment was growing apace. By 1969 it had utterly abandoned its old role of blackening the wings of moths and was now conterminous with the British Isles and their surrounding seas. By 1970 it was lapping the shores of the United States. Inevitably, instead of influencing others it became itself subject to almost intolerable pressures. Things were thrown into it. 'An estimated 160 million pounds of mercury,' declared *The Times* in a Christmas message about poisoned fish, 'has been dumped in the environment this century.' The boot was now on the other leg with a vengeance. With its mastery over human and animal life almost entirely gone, the Environment had become something to be saved, and the British Government, in what looked like a last desperate throw, appointed a Secretary of State for it.

This was a far cry from flannel waistcoats and the old snug personal cocoon to which everyone, moth or man, used to have a right. Nothing seemed to be left to blame for one's own individual failures or successes, happiness or misery, but poor old neglected heredity – for which at the moment of writing not even a Royal Commission has been appointed.

The hideous thing, one of the hideous things, about this new Environment is that it is so convenient. Indeed, it may have been touch and go whether we had a Minister for the Convenience. 'The Environment' is all-embracing – except that it has no people in it. There is no need to define what you are talking about. There is the word, a nice, solid, official-sounding sort of word, and something must obviously correspond with it. It is the kind of word that goes well with cost-benefit analyses. It saves the endless fatigue of acquainting yourself with all the minutiae that make up a countryside, all the real personal environments that constitute the stuff of life. It is as handily soulless as, for instance, that Area 26 into which a part of my own county is to be gloriously translated ('Come on, Area 26', I hear myself shouting at some inter-environmental Rugby football match of the future. 'Shove this damned Conurbation off it!') It is too grandiose a conception, stuffed as it is with mercury and oil-rigs, to concern itself with what matters to us, here in a small village that does not even boast an Environment officer.

What does matter, environmentally, to the individual? There reached me, rather surprisingly, some months ago a letter from Lincoln First Banks, Inc, of Rochester, NY (addressed to me as 'a member of the communications industry' – which is no bad thing to be; old members, Shakespeare and Tolstoi, to name but two). 'Lincoln First Banks', they singularly wrote, 'is very much concerned about tomorrow and has undertaken a serious study into the American life styles which might be anticipated in the 1980s. The objective of the research has been to look at *the individual* ten years from now, and *all of the forces affecting him to make up his total environment*'.

This was cheering. Here was an organisation prepared, as is clear from the words I have taken the liberty of italicising, to recognise the existence of individuals, each with his own environment, and to show confidence, what is more, that the same state of affairs would last for at least another decade. And how did Lincoln First Banks define or classify the 'forces affecting'?

'The study profile,' they wrote, 'was divided into twelve sub-topics – The Qualitative Life Style; Population; Employment; Sustenance; Housing and Construction; Transportation and Communication; Health; Education; Social Structures; Ecology; Government; Culture/Recreation/Entertainment'.

Well, that adds up to quite an environment. Obviously very different from that formless expanding affair with the definite article, to which I take such grave exception. Even so it does not sound quite the personal environment I hanker after. It is not cosy enough. It lacks warmth. I have difficulty in squeezing into any of the twelve categories some of the forces that particularly affect me here. We have Transportation in the village, and Government naturally, and Social Structures, if that is what the Parish Hall is; but it is none of these that has incised the calipers so deeply from my nose to my chin. It is old Mrs Barstow and her dogs. Nor can my characteristic (certainly not inherited) of darting down side roads whenever Colonel Curtis comes along be properly entered under Recreation.

What I am trying to say is that, if Lincoln First Banks were to extend their survey across the Atlantic and happened to call at my house for information, the details of my environment that I should wish to stress, the forces that really affect me for good or ill, would not fit very readily into their Study Profile – or that of any other praiseworthy sociologist. Ground elder could, I suppose, come at a pinch under Ecology, but to attempt to subsume the milkman's gay errors under Sustenance or Mrs Barstow under Culture or Entertainment, either now or in ten years' time, would be to make a mockery of serious research. Or is it possible that both these dear people, and the rats in the outhouse, and the view from my bedroom window, and the gurglings made by our vertically distintegrated central-heating system, and Matins, and Colonel Curtis, and the delicious row in the Debating Society, and a hundred other vital ingredients in the environment of myself and my neighbours all make up our Qualitative Life Style?

I cannot say; as yet, for all our amenities, we have no such thing in the village. What I can say is that this sort of personal and priceless environment is not going to be saved, or even comprehended, by any Secretary of State, born or unborn. We have to do that ourselves.

Threnody for Thirty Thousand Butlers

1981

Butlers are becoming rare. Today there are said to be 'only about one hundred' in all Britain, and that I can easily believe, whereas – the astonishing statement leaps out at me from the columns of a dependable English newspaper – 'before the war Britain boasted 30,000 of them.' The word 'boasted' is perhaps ill-chosen; we did not as a nation, so far as my experience goes, make much of a song in the nervous thirties about this remarkable figure, nor did we attempt to impress Hitler with the strength of these hidden reserves. But that is beside the point. It is the figure itself on which I wish to dwell.

There are aggregates, immensities, imponderables even, in the face of which my imagination has learned, as the years go by, not to flinch. Astronomical numbers, say. If I am told that such-and-such a galaxy is a million light-years away, I can shrug it off with ease, whether or no I take the trouble to multiply the million by one hundred and eighty-six thousand times three hundred and sixty-five times twenty-four times sixty times sixty in order to render the thing down into miles. It is the same with the number of molecules in a cubic centimetre of gas, which for the moment I forget. I can also visualise enormous masses of Chinese or Iranians, perhaps aided by the fact that I often see half a million or so of them on my television screen, carrying baskets of earth on their heads or shaking their fists in the air, as the case may be. But thirty thousand butlers are a different kettle of fish. The spectacle of such a multitude, in sombre tailcoated array, on (let us say) a protest march through Hyde Park is one that I cannot by any stretch of the imagination encompass. Why, if they were ranged in columns of threes and we allowed them one yard between ranks, I calculate the procession would cover the best part of six miles from head to tail, and, at two miles per hour, which is a gait your trained butler never permits himself to exceed, would take some three hours to pass the reviewing stand.

This failure of the imagination I put down to the very nature of butlerdom. Butlers are solitary; they never flock. They come as single spies, not in battalions. They stand alone – or used to stand – at the portals of their thirty thousand individual mansions, overseeing the arrival or, with backward-curved right hand, the departure of innumerable distinguished guests. To picture them in groups, even in pairs, is to do violence to their very essence. The two-butler household, though conceivable perhaps in Texas, is a phenomenon unheard of in these British islands even at the peak of our prosperity. An under-butler, it is true, is occasionally mentioned in the literature dealing with the organisation and management of great houses, but him and his title I regard as no more than a piece of self-aggrandisement on the part of his employer; his duties, it seems to me, are indistinguishable from those of a senior footman. Your true, your veritable, butler can no more be duplicated – at his duties in the wine cellar, in his pantry, when announcing dinner, or taking his place behind his master's chair (on the left, mind) – than can an archbishop at a coronation.

You did not know that a butler's place at the beginning of dinner is behind his master's chair, on the *left*? There is no need to feel ashamed. I should not have known it myself, so far removed has my life been spent from the more delicate nuances of meals in good society, had not the great *Mrs Beeton's Book of Household Management* (edition of 1909) been for so many years constantly at my elbow. When I was a child, the colour plates were perhaps my favourite study, and even now I cannot look with indifference at 'Household Utensils' (facing page 80, and including Wringer and Mangle, in red and green, and a very fine rotating Knife Cleaner embellished with the royal arms) or the double-page 'Dinner Table, à la Russe' (between pages 1552 and 1553), with its pink-shaded candelabra; its massed chrysanthemums and delicate fronds of greenery trailing down at the four corners, to set off the dozen double-damask dinner napkins, each ingeniously folded to encapsulate its enticing bread roll; the guest cards cut to resemble shallops, dhows, or some Russian equivalent in full sail; the inimitable cruets; and the forty-eight wineglasses – that's only four per person, as may be readily reckoned – disposed so neatly to the side (the *right* side, naturally) of their relevant setting. A picture to set the gastric juices flowing, if ever there was one – and there are plenty in Mrs Beeton's book; the halibut facing page 289 is masterly.

For serious reading, however, we must press on to page 1763, where the 'domestic duties of the butler' are faithfully set down:

At dinner, he places the silver and plated articles on the table, and sees that everything is in its place. Where the dishes are carved on the dinner table he carries in the first dish, and announces in the drawing-room that dinner is on the table, and respectfully stands by the door until the company are seated, when he takes his place behind his master's chair on the left, to remove the covers, handing them to the other attendants to carry out. After the first course of plates is supplied, his place is at the sideboard to serve the wines, but only when called on. The first course ended. . . .

But enough. The realisation that all over Britain, in the heyday of this country and its butlery, at eight o'clock in the evening precisely, thirty thousand butlers were taking their places behind their masters' chairs (on the *left*), removing the covers and handing them to the other attendants – this is a thought that comes near to paralysing the mind with wonder. I see them as in a kind of dream; portly, swallow-tailed, full-cheeked, balding and benign, a little bowed, a little stertorous perhaps (for even butlers must breathe) – though not, one likes to think, actually wheezing. I see this vast but fragmented army moving as one man from behind their masters' chairs toward the myriad sideboards, there to wait, patiently but not, no doubt, in vain, until called on.

The picture is perhaps a little overdrawn. Butlers, when they pullulated like flies, can hardly have been cast all in the same traditional mould. The stout and stately figure of my dreams, the Platonic ideal of a butler, derived, I daresay, largely from such creations as P.G. Wodehouse's butler Beach (see the Blandings Castle novels *passim*), has, on inspection, to undergo some modification. Not all butlers, it seems, were always portly, benign, or even (I blush to report it) as respectful as Mrs Beeton and I would wish. There is that story – not, I believe, apocryphal – of the old butler whose demeanour at a grand dinner party was so markedly unbalanced that his mistress (was it Lady Astor?) felt impelled to scribble down and hand to him the curt message 'Leave the room immediately. You are drunk.' After the briefest glance at this instruction, the butler moved down the table and laid it, with, one feels sure, some return of his smoothest manner, before the astounded eyes of (I think) Sir John Simon.

Well, if that was his final act of butlery, one has to admit it showed a certain flair. But listen to what Max Beerbohm, that old favourite of mine, had to say in an essay on 'Servants', written as long ago as 1918.

I have seen, from time to time, butlers who had shed all semblance of grace, butlers whose whole demeanour was a manifesto of contempt for their calling and of devotion to the Spirit of the Age. I have seen a butler in a well-established household strolling around the diners without the slightest droop, and pouring out wine in an off-hand and quite obviously hostile manner. I have seen him, towards the end of the meal, yawning. I remember another whom, positively, I heard humming – a faint sound indeed, but menacing as the roll of tumbrils.

These, of course, were exceptional cases, as Beerbohm grants; among a host of thirty thousand, one or two backsliders were, I suppose, to be expected, and I cling to the hope, I am surely entitled to believe, that in the ranks of the pitiful one hundred or so butlers still left to us no single renegade is to be found – that they are, one and all, the finest flower of butlerdom: all portly, all drooping slightly, every man of them prepared to stand as respectfully by the dining-room door as their forerunners when the century was young.

That new recruits to the profession will attain the highest standards of the past we can at least be assured. That same dependable newspaper of which I made mention at the start informs me that a School for British Butlers opened at Belair Mansion, Dulwich, on 29 December last, under the control of toastmaster Mr Ivor Spencer, and with Mr Leslie Bartlett, 'professional butler to royalty' and a mature sixty-eight-year-old (no hummer he, we may be sure), as chief instructor. This is to be no harum-scarum affair, no crash course in cover-removing, with just a couple of days devoted to the care of wines. 'Discretion and dedication,' Mr Bartlett declares, are to be the hallmark, and he 'plans to enrol only two prospective butlers per 18-month course,' thus ensuring the closest personal supervision and an end product of which this country may assuredly in due time be proud.

Proud of, yes, but not, I fear, benefited by. An output of two butlers every eighteen months is hardly calculated to swell appreciably Great Britain's modest tally of butlers, in whose drooping ranks wastage must inevitably be high, and even those two are unlikely to take their places behind British chairs. For, so I read, 'Wealthy American bankers and show business personalities [a plague on both their households] are already queuing up for the finished Jeeves [*sic*] product.' Let them queue. They are in for a long wait, let me tell them – and longer still before their prized School graduate turns into the butler of their dreams. You can teach a man to stand respectfully at door or sideboard, to pour out wine, to perform with address and skill the multifarious duties of a butler in a well-established household, but only time can fill out his waistcoat, bow his shoulders, remove a sufficiency of hair, and in general lend him that air of loyal and dignified benevolence without which even a dinner table à la Russe lacks the final touch of distinction. And the first pupil enrolled at the School for British Butlers, you wealthy bankers may as well know, is aged sixteen at the time of writing. I reckon he should attain the full flower of butlerdom in or around the year 2025.

It only remains for me to withdraw an adjective twice employed, ill-advisedly and prematurely, above. A newspaper capable of confusing a valet, or gentleman's gentleman, with a butler would not be described either by Beach or by Mrs Beeton, and least of all by Jeeves himself, as 'dependable.'

The Naked-Ape Crisis

1968

This is a last-ditch attempt to differentiate myself from a ten-spined stickleback. The thing began when naturalists grew tired of shooting and stuffing the creatures they loved, or pinning them in rows in glass cases, and began peering at them instead in the wild state. Fabre spied on beetles. Eliot Howard spent a lifetime watching warblers through binoculars and came up with his theory of bird territory. Julian Huxley observed crested grebes as they had never been observed before. Konrad Lorenz kept a close eye on jackdaws, geese, and dogs. Niko Tinbergen enlisted in a herring-full colony. Soon there was scarcely a bird, an ape, a gazelle, a dragonfly whose bowings and scrapings, preening, threats, empurplings, and sac-swellings were not being observed somewhere by somebody. Amid the welter of head-noddings and twig-fiddlings thus brought to light, it was natural that certain resemblances between animal and human behaviour should be noted. When a gull pulls furiously at grass because (so they say) it is frustrated by two antagonistic drives, its affinity with a man who lights a cigarette while trying to decide between Scotch and bourbon is fairly clear.

It had not at this stage been suggested that because Horace Walpole decorated Strawberry Hill with colourful Gothic bric-a-brac he was practically indistinguishable from a bower-bird. The differences between man and beast were at first apparent even to the animal-behaviour observers, or ethologists, who were at pains to remind their readers that animals were not human. 'Let us have none of this anthropomorphism!' they cried, carefully putting quotation marks around any tiresomely humanoid words like 'affection', 'cruel', or 'happy' that had crept unawares into their texts. As recently as 1953, Tinbergen was writing, 'It is scarcely necessary to stress the differences in type of organisation between human societies and those of gulls.'

It is highly necessary now. Scarcely had these ethologists finished shaking their fingers at sentimentalists who spoke of animals as though they were men when they themselves set to work to prove that men were animals. Zoomorphism became rife. Mr Robert Ardrey has devoted a whole book to it, coming up with the conclusion that the Italian lives in a *noyau* and bases his home life on that of the sportive lemur, whereas the American, at home in a nation, is more of a howling monkey. Mr Ardrey himself, when engulfed at the time of Pearl Harbour in a wave of patriotic fervour, hardly knew whether he was a chacma baboon or a roebuck. Zoologist Dr Desmond Morris, whose book about men, *The Naked Ape*, has lately appeared, seems to be in hardly better case. 'The book,' he has explained to an interviewer, 'deals with sex, fighting, feeding, parental care, exploration, and comfort. They're exactly the same chapter headings used for my thesis on the Ten-Spined Stickleback. I wanted to demonstrate how alike we all are in certain respects.'

I shall not read it. Though I prefer to do my fighting and feeding without constantly comparing myself with a stickleback, these sociological generalisations do not especially alarm me. If it is Mr Ardrey's territorial imperative that urges me and the rest of my troop to defend ourselves, or if I am called upon, as indicated by Dr Lorenz, to discharge my aggressive drives after the manner of a dabbling duck, I shall not make an issue of it. It is in the particulars of behaviour, rather than the general, that I wish to dissociate myself from the animal kingdom.

'It is tempting,' writes Dr Lorenz, 'to interpret the

greeting smile [in man] as an appeasing ceremony which . . . has evolved by ritualization of redirected threatening. The friendly tooth-baring of very polite Japanese lends support to this theory. It is also supported by the fact that in genuinely emotional intensive greetings between two friends, the smile surprisingly becomes a loud laugh. On considering one's own feelings it seems incongruous that, on meeting a friend after a long separation, the roar of laughter breaks forth unexpectedly from the depths of instinctive strata of our personality. This behaviour of two reunited human beings must inevitably remind an objective behaviour investigator of the triumph ceremony of greylag geese.'

I have not had the good fortune to be present when Dr Lorenz meets an old friend after a long separation, and cannot tell whether I should be objective enough to be reminded of greylag geese. But I am by no means ready, on the available evidence, to have the smiles of my friends written off as redirected threatening. If the good Doctor had made as intensive a study of long-lost friends as he has of geese, I would give him best. But has he? Ethologists do not dream of making assertions, drawing conclusions, evolving theories about baboons, or even three-spined sticklebacks without prolonged observation and experiment. They put rats in mazes and make oyster-catchers sit on square eggs. I have not heard of similar work being done on Italians or old friends. I myself once broke into loud laughter on meeting a brother after years of separation. But there was an extraneous factor, which seemed to me to eliminate my instinctive strata. His face, after a lengthy tour in West Africa, had become unexpectedly round and red, and upon this tropical moon he had chosen to perch a small brown trilby hat. Dr Lorenz had not thought of that. He had better put a small brown hat on a greylag goose and see what sort of triumph ceremony that evokes.

The horse in my paddock inclines its ears toward me when I call but promptly flicks one of them to the north-north-east if some more interesting sound, such as a power mower, starts up. A Mrs Dinwiddy, to whom I sometimes speak at sherry parties, undeniably listens with at least one ear to what the couple behind us are saying. An ethologist would at once dismiss her as a horse. But she is not. The point I wish to emphasise, before man has been stripped of every vestige of dignity, is that her ears remain stationary throughout. This lack of overt physical response to stimuli is the shining glory of the human race. We must cling to it.

What is urgently wanted is a close study of human behaviour designed to demonstrate how unlike ring-tailed lemurs we all are in certain respects. It must be undertaken by a man objective enough to seek out behavioural norms before leaping to conclusions. He will have a job on his hands, though. It is a great deal more difficult to observe our own species, or order, under the proper conditions than it is to watch lemurs or owls. I had just got my wickerwork blind erected in one of London's public parks, waved goodbye to my assistant, and settled down to watch the behaviour patterns of urban courting couples when a helmet was pushed through the flap and its owner asked me what I thought I was up to. With crested grebes, if two persons enter a blind and one goes away, the birds are satisfied and resume their occupations. But policemen can count. So valuable time had to be wasted while I tried to explain the urgent need for statistical proof that the human race, ethologically speaking, differs markedly from the rest of the animal kingdom. 'For instance, the ruff,' I told him, 'when ready to mate, turns white, black, purple, chestnut, or buff round the neck, and develops uncouth ear tufts. I expect to show that that is an awkwardness from which Londoners, in normal circumstances, are free.'

'Is that so?' he said.

'Yes,' I said. 'And what's more, the head of the North African freshwater fish *Tilapia zillii* becomes velvet black at such times, with turquoise spots, while the throat and chest turn blood red. Even if some ethologists may conceivably be reminded—'

'Binoculars, too, I see,' the officer said, making a note of it.

'Naturally. You may not be aware that the American sage grouse, by expansion and contraction of the neck-sacs during courting, produces a sound that can be heard a mile away on a still morning. For comparative purposes, it is essential to be able to carry out long-range observations. After eating eels—'

'Shocking, this is,' he said. 'Peeping Tom. It's an offence.'

I had been about to tell him, as a further instance of the kind of behaviour rarely found in human beings, whether courting or not, that the common heron, *Ardea cinerea*, removes eel slime from its plumage by sprinkling its head and shoulders with a kind of powder secreted in a pocket near the base of the tail. But it was clear by this time that he was the sort of man hardly worth distinguishing from an animal. You get these zoomorphic freaks. 'For example,' I said instead, trying to find a homelier example, 'when feeding her young, does your wife regurgitate half-digested fish?'

He turned so extraordinary a colour round the neck that a less objective observer might have supposed he was ready to mate. But I have been long enough at the game to recognise aggression when I see it, whether in stickleback or man. We now had an almost perfect set-up for a demonstration of the territorial imperative. The blind was my territory, and so long as I was in it I *must* be the dominant individual. The policeman, however, had pretty obviously never read Mr Ardrey, so I took to my heels. This proves, I think, that I am less of a chacma baboon than some other ethologists I could name.

The Last Repository

Of the mental exercises, or fantasies, I indulge in to keep myself awake when I cannot sleep, perhaps, the most useless runs as follows: I am the last adult on earth, in charge of a huddle of children who will be the fathers and mothers of all future mankind. We are in some sort of safe place and have no immediate problems about survival or keeping out the rain. I don't know how we got there and I don't care, any more than I concern myself with the details of our daily life. I am too old now to picture myself as the kind of man who could carve fish-hooks out of bones in an emergency. All that side of life is somehow provided for; nor am I answerable to anyone for a full explanation. If I were cooking up an imaginative novel, it would be different; fiction is sacred, fantasy is free. So, also, I am not compelled to account to myself for the fact that all knowledge has disappeared along with my contemporaries. All books, all instruments and apparatus, all drugs, vehicles, weapons, factories, pots, pans, and other relics of civilization have been destroyed or buried irretrievably under a thick layer of radioactive dust. I am the sole repository of the accumulated wisdom and experience of man, from pre-Sumerian times to the holocaust.

I feel the responsibility acutely, and often have to turn my pillow over to keep a cool head when I reflect that whatever I fail to pass on to my little band of orphans tumbling about so happily in the sun will be lost forever – or at best will have to be rediscovered by the slow and painful process of trial and error. It seems to me a terrible thing that the human race should have to wait another seven thousand years before safety matches are available again. I cannot bear to contemplate the repetition of the myriad ingenious fallacies and misapprehensions that have bedevilled the course of human history. It was some five thousand years after the dawn of civilization (which I take leave to date around the sixth millennium) before Empedocles produced the notion that earth, air, fire, and water were the four elements of which everything was composed, and got considerable credit for this error. More than two thousand years later, imponderables like phlogiston, caloric, and ether were still supposed to be at large in the universe, accounting for things. We do not want to plough our way through all that stuff again. And only I, tossing can turning in my lonely bed, can prevent it.

I must try to put my toddlers on the right lines about protons and neutrons, which is bound to involve some preliminary talk about electricity. And this again reminds me that I may not be spared long enough for their tiny minds to be ready for instruction about even so elementary a matter as winding wire around a magnetised iron core. I may be suffering from a touch of strontium 90, which could be a serious thing at my age. In case anything irremediable happens to me in the meantime, I ought to write these things down. I have paper and pencils in this fantasy, for I really cannot be bothered to improvise clay tablets at half past one in the morning. But what shall I write? Where shall I begin my task? The phrase 'something irremediable' that came into my head just now is a pleasant Grecism for death and reminds me that the achievement of ancient Athens will be lost forever unless I put it down on paper. It is a question of time and evaluation. I find it extraordinarily difficult to decide whether Sophocles or safety matches should come first.

'Safety matches are a simple means of producing fire and are made by dipping thin pieces of wood into a brown mixture containing phosphorus,' I see myself jotting down for posterity. 'When the brown end is rubbed against some more of this brown stuff, a flame results and the piece of wood burns. Phosphorus is found in bones, if I remember rightly, and you will just have to keep on trying until you learn how to extract it.'

This, to my surprise, is the best note I can write about the manufacture of matches without getting out of bed and consulting an encyclopedia. I should be sounder on Sophocles, I think, but it is hard to believe that a people still at the stage of rubbing sticks together would have time for Greek tragedy. I am constantly up against this problem of priorities. I desperately want, for instance, to give them a glimmering about airplanes, not caring to think about lives uselessly thrown away two thousand years hence in experiments with canvas frameworks attached to the arms. But it would be a long business, and at the end of it I doubt whether a machine made to my instructions would be stable in a high wind. How is it to be powered? I daresay I could set down the princple of the internal combustion engine in terms that would save time for these youngsters, once they had found out how to make steel, and I could add a footnote about jet propulsion for later on. It is the thought of the fuel that depresses me. When the whole human race is numbered in tens, or even in thousands, how does one present to them in an attractive light, as a worthwhile operation, the process of drilling tremendously deep holes in the earth on the off chance of finding a substance that is useless until you have cracked it?

I am up against much the same difficulty over drip-dry shirts. The truth seems to be that you have to have a population running into millions before anyone will take the trouble to make machines capable of producing millions of shirts. This is the kind of hard economic fact one comes up against around 3 a.m., when it begins to look as if the first essential step to be taken by my little group of survivors on the road back to civilization is to multiply as rapidly as possible. I do not feel, however, that I need give them any guidance about that.

Sometimes, at about this point in my fantasy, I half decide to concentrate on culture, eked out with a few simple conveniences made of wood. Aristotle's definition of tragedy; whatever of Shakespeare I have by heart; the principle of the lever; the golden section, if I can be sure of it; a rough sketch of a wheelbarrow – that would not be a contemptible contribution to the future of the race. I could add an appendix stating a few scientific facts (the sun is ninety-three million miles away; water boils at two hundred and twelve degrees Fahrenheit) for them to make what they liked of. But I can't be satisfied with it. There is a sense of waste, of irreparable loss. Before long I am stuck again with the old desire to give them *all* I know, convinced anew that I must take the long-term view, that in the long run the merest hint – a shadowy clue about the possibility of refrigeration, pneumatic tyres, anaesthetics, the telephone, dried milk – is better than the endless silence of the tomb. Am I to lie here like a hog, sheltering behind the lateness of the hour, and deprive millions yet unborn of the knowledge that trees cut up fine, boiled into a mash, and rolled out thin can be written on with ink?

I am now face to face with the appalling truth that I have no idea how ink is made. Is it conceivable that it is still harvested from deliberately frightened cuttlefish on extensive squid farms? If so, I shall never touch it again.

The danger of setting down information for a too distant posterity is that it may be disregarded in the meantime – even lost – or its purpose may be misconceived. I foresee, as the cocks begin to crow, the possibility that my notebooks, with their fragments of Tennyson's 'Ulysses', their squiggled representations of sewing machines and teapots, the brave attempt at the binomial theorem, will within a few generations assume the status of legend, become the corpus of a world mythology. My notebooks may, though I rather hope not, found a new religion. My description of the random behaviour of molecules in an expanded gas may be read out on feast days by some uncomprehending priest while the multitude prostrates itself in awe and terror.

This is a risk that I am prepared to take. Justice will in the end be done. Some Schliemann of the future, filled with burning faith, will unearth with his primitive spade the proof that my writings are as true as Homer's. 'I have gazed,' he will report in a dramatic smoke signal, 'upon the veritable egg whisk of the Notebooks.' This will cause a proper stir. The knowledge that the Notebooks are not Myth but Manual is bound to change the course of history. The tribe or clan that owns them, with the secret of the spoked wheel safe in its grasp, must inevitably predominate. My book will become the Book of Power – closely guarded, eagerly sought, probably fought for. The thought that my patient labour may well become the cause of World War IV sometimes, though not invariably, sends me to sleep.